About the author

Evelyn Findlater started to incorporate more natural foods into her family's diet when she was a mother at Teacher Training College. She found there were few books giving information on how to cook these foods well and even fewer stimulating recipes. She later started her own healthfood shop which she ran for four years – customers loved all the healthfood and asked if she would give wholefood cookery classes, which she did. The response was terrific and the classes stimulated her to write her first book, *Wholefood Cookery Course*. She has since written several cookery books including *Making Your Own Proteins* and *Off the Shelf* (both published by Century) and appears regularly on television.

The Natural Entertainer

The Natural Entertainer

THE HEALTHY WAY TO DELICIOUS FOOD

Evelyn Findlater

CENTURY
LONDON MELBOURNE AUCKLAND JOHANNESBURG

Copyright © EVELYN FINDLATER 1987

First published in 1987 by Century Hutchinson Ltd
Brookmount House, 62–65 Chandos Place
London WC2N 4NW

Century Hutchinson Australia (Pty) Ltd
PO Box 496, 16–22 Church Street
Hawthorn, Victoria 3122
Australia

Century Hutchinson New Zealand Ltd
PO Box 40–086, 32–34 View Road
Glenfield, Auckland 10
New Zealand

Century Hutchinson South Africa (Pty) Ltd
PO Box 337, Bergvlei
South Africa

Cover illustration by Jane Strother
Illustrated by Paul Davies

Set by Deltatype, Ellesmere Port

Printed and bound in Great Britain
by The Guernsey Press Co Ltd, Guernsey, Channel Islands

British Library Cataloguing in Publication Data

Findlater, Evelyn
    The Natural Entertainer : the healthy
    way to delicious food.
    1. Cookery (Natural foods) 2. Entertaining
    I. Title
    641.5'68   TX741

    ISBN 0–7126–1619–5

Contents

Introduction

This book is about entertaining for pleasure with healthy foods that are not only beautifully presented but taste absolutely delicious. It is for vegetarians who do not eat meat or fish, for vegans who eat neither meat, fish or dairy produce, and for meat lovers who can eat the lot.

No matter which diet you choose, whether it is vegetarian, vegan or meat-eating, it can be a healthy one. Our Western diet, which is said to contain too much meat, saturated fats, sugar and salt and not enough fibre, has taken a huge hammering in the last few years. It is becoming increasingly evident that our pattern of eating in the West is a major factor in causing diseases which are comparatively unknown in societies which have a completely different diet. However, this does not mean that we have to change all our eating habits overnight. Drastically cutting down or out foods without knowing which alternatives to introduce can be dangerous to our health. It is important to learn how to combine unfamiliar foods in order to create a well balanced diet which contains the essential nutrients vital for health.

Entertaining, even small numbers, can be daunting and positively nerve-racking if you are trying out new dishes with unusual ingredients for the first time. However, you don't have to wait for these occasions to experiment with new foods. The information which follows about the ingredients will help you to succeed in preparing any of the dishes in the menus whenever you feel like cooking creatively, whether it be for family or friends, or both.

Happy, healthy eating.

About the Ingredients

Before I started 13 years ago to think about eating for health as well as enjoyment, I followed recipes which tasted and looked good, added my own touch here and there and felt very creative. Although fresh fruit, vegetables, herbs and spices have always figured prominently in my cooking, flour and rice were definitely white, the only other grains I used were porridge oats and pearl barley. My only knowledge of pulses was that lentils or split peas added flavour and thickened my soups and meat was usually consumed twice daily.

Today, not only are we fortunate enough to be able to choose from a huge variety of imported foods from all parts of the globe but also we can enjoy the superb cuisine created in the countries from where these ingredients originate. Many of the ingredients I have used in the book are now easily available in most healthfood stores and some supermarkets. The following information will tell you how to balance certain foods to make a complete protein (see pages 19–24), their nutritional value and, in some cases, how to grow or make them.

All-Year-Round Bean and Seed Sprout Salad

This wonderful all-year-round salad is now easily available in 275g (10 oz) packs and is usually grown from mung beans (see page 20). However, it is very easy to grow using a variety of beans and seeds which in my opinion have much more flavour than the commercial variety.

When sprouted the beans and seeds increase enormously in food value. The proteins, carbohydrates and oils break down into more digestible amino acids, natural sugars and fatty acids and there is a considerable increase in the quantity of vitamin and amino acids (see page 20) already present in the dormant seed.

Here I will give you basic instructions on how to sprout some of my favourite beans and seeds. Just 50g (2 oz) beans and seeds will produce 225g (8 oz) when sprouted. All you will need is a good size glass jar with a wide rim, a piece of muslin and an elastic band.

Wash the beans and seeds and soak for the given length of time (see below), drain, place in the clean jar, cover the opening with the muslin and secure this with an elastic band. Place the jar on its side out of direct sunlight and in an approximate temperature of 30°c to 35°c (65°F to 70°F). Rinse by pouring cold water gently through the muslin then carefully drain all the water out through the muslin.

For Sprouting Soya Beans: Soak for 12 hours, rinse 4 times daily. Take 5 days to sprout (see page 162 for Sprouted Soya Bean Purée).
For Sprouting Mung Beans: Soak for 12 hours, rinse 3 times daily. Take 5 days to sprout.
For Sprouting Whole Lentils: Soak for 8 hours, rinse 3 times daily. Take 4 days to sprout. (Split lentils will not sprout.)
For Sprouting Alfalfa Seeds: Soak for 6 hours, rinse 3 times daily. Take 5 days to sprout.
Note: Alfalfa seeds when sprouted contain 40% protein, are very rich in vitamins and minerals and have the same amount of carotene as carrots. The sprouts are thin and curl around each other in a light bundle so they are excellent in sandwiches and look great as a healthy frilly garnish to any salad or main dish.

Herbs (grown indoors)

You can buy good quality dried herbs but I don't think you can beat the flavour of fresh ones. So, why not grow your own indoors and have fresh herbs all the year round? Besides being useful they smell beautiful and make very decorative house plants. I have a shelf arrangement in front of the sunniest window in the house and arrange my pots on there. They thrive in a warm place in the sun. They do not like highly centrally heated houses or hot air currents. The ideal temperature is between 24°c/30°c (50°F/60°F). When the weather turns very cold insulate the window on frosty nights by covering the glass with a sheet of polythene or move the plants into the room.

You can buy packets of seeds which state 'suitable for growing indoors'. Follow the instructions on the packet. However, I suggest you buy small bushy, not thin and spindly plants if you are a real beginner. Remember that an annual lasts 1 year, a biennial 2 years and a perennial several years.

Personally I think the most useful are basil (my favourite and most delicate annual), parsley (biennial), chives, thyme and marjoram (all perennial), but there are lots of others to choose from.

Some plants will need re-potting straight away if they are extra thick. To do this tilt the pot, tap to release the root from the soil, put a layer of stones at the bottom of your next-size-up pot, and then a thick layer of good potting compost. Gently press in the root of the plant then press more compost around and over it. Use tepid water to moisten lightly and keep in a shaded place for a few days so that the plant gets used to its environment. Then put on display in the window.

Taking care of your herbs is vital. Moisten with tepid water every 2 days when growing vigorously in the summer and every 5 days in the winter. The soil must not be too wet, just dampish. (I use any left-over herb teas to water my plants.) Once every 2 weeks feed them with liquid fertilizer (following the instructions on the bottle) and occasionally use an atomizer to spray with water so that the leaves keep clean. I can assure you all this is well worth your care and effort. You have food, scent and house plants all in one.

Herb Vinegars and Oils

Herb oils and vinegars are delicious in salad dressings and marinades. Choose tarragon, basil and dill for 3 beautiful herb-flavoured oils and vinegars.

To 275ml (1 pint) cold-pressed olive or sunflower oil or 275ml (1 pint) light cider or wine vinegar add 3 heaped teaspoons of the slightly bruised leaves of either of the herbs mentioned above. Stir, bottle and cork tightly. Let the oil and herb infuse for 2 to 3 weeks and the vinegar and herb for 1 week to 10 days. Shake from time to time. Strain and pour into clean bottles adding just 1 sprig of the herb before corking very tightly.

Note: You can freeze the oil with the bruised herb leaves in small containers without leaving to infuse or straining. When defrosted the flavour is superb and will excite any salad dressing.

How to Make Fruit Vinegars

For these you can use a good wine or light cider vinegar. They will be ready in 2 days and, after straining and bottling, will last for several months or longer. I have not used these vinegars extensively through the book because there is nothing more irritating than wanting to do a recipe and finding that one of the ingredients is not obtainable in the shops or you can't make it quickly. If you can spare the time, fruit vinegars are well worth making and storing for use in salads and marinades.

To every 275ml (1 pint) white wine or light cider vinegar you will need 225g (8 oz) soft fruit such as raspberries, ripe pears, simply chopped with skins on; red currants, taken off stems and pressed very, very gently with a potato masher; peaches, chopped, apricots, chopped or mangos, chopped. Put the fruit of your choice into a bowl, washing it well before chopping or pressing. Pour on the wine or light cider vinegar. Stir well and cover with foil and a towel and leave for 2 days. Put the lot into a saucepan and bring to boiling point. Strain and pour the fruity vinegar liquid into sterilized bottles. Cork or secure tightly with screw tops. Use as you would plain vinegar for the most delicious added flavour to your salads or marinades.

Oils and Fats

The best oils for health and flavour are undoubtedly cold-pressed or virgin vegetable-based oils, high in polyunsaturates, where the seeds are not subjected to heat in order to extract the oil from them.

Polyunsaturated Fats are high in linoleic acid which helps control the level of cholesterol in the blood. These include safflower seed oil (highest in linoleic acid), sunflower oil, corn oil, soya oil, sesame seed oil and some margarines marked high in polyunsaturates. The deliciously flavoured olive oil marked 'extra virgin' which is a green colour, contains mono-unsaturated fatty acids which do not contribute to heart disease. Although it is low in linoleic acid this oil increases the absorption of vitamins, A, D, E and K and is easily digestible. So, lovers of this oil can all breathe a sigh of relief.

Saturated Fats if eaten in large amounts produce high levels of cholesterol in the blood which is now generally accepted as making us more vulnerable, not only to heart attacks, but also to thrombosis, gall stones, and associated illnesses. These fats include: all animal fats, such as lard, cheese, butter and cream; palm oil and some vegetable fats; margarines (see below), unless marked high in polyunsaturates.

Margarines: Most margarines are hydrogenated (chemically hardened), which is the process used to create a texture for spreading. This process of hydrogenation changes polyunsaturated fats into saturated fats. Fats chemically altered in this way can make essential fatty acids unavailable to the body. There are however, one or two margarines on the market which do not go through this chemical process and are produced naturally with cold-pressed polyunsaturated oils. Vitaquell is one of these delicious and healthy margarines.

Yoghurt

Real yoghurt is made with two live cultures, *Lactobacillus bulgaricus* and *Streptococcus thermophilus*. The bacteria in live yoghurt kills harmful bacteria in our bodies. It turns milk sugar (lactose) into lactic acid in which harmful bacteria cannot live. The beneficial bacteria in live yoghurt can also manufacture (produce) the B vitamins in our bodies. For those of you who are taking antibiotics, which are known to cause vitamin deficiency, eating about 300ml (½ pint) yoghurt daily will help to keep this vital vitamin in the body.

Yoghurt is very easy to make. A yoghurt maker simplifies matters, but wrapping a towel several layers thick around the container and placing it on a radiator or in an airing cupboard will give you lovely yoghurt in about 7 hours. If you want thickish yoghurt then simply add 2 tablespoons of skimmed milk powder to 275ml (1 pint) milk just before adding the culture.

You can make yoghurt with cow's, goat's or unsweetened soya milk. You can also thicken soya milk yoghurt by adding 2 tablespoons soya milk powder to the soya milk just before adding the culture (see other references to soya milk yoghurt, page 17).

For perfection use a thermometer to test the temperature of the milk and sterilize the container.

Bring 900ml (1½ pints) milk to the boil, take off heat and leave to cool to a temperature of 43°c (110°F). If you want thick yoghurt then stir in the milk powder. Add 2 generous tablespoons of natural live yoghurt (look at the labels; stabilizers and sweeteners kill live yoghurt). Whisk well and pour into a warm container or your yoghurt maker. Wrap in a warm towel if you have no yoghurt maker and keep in a warm place either on a radiator or in a warm airing cupboard. Leave to stand for 5 to 7 hours. Refrigerate and the yoghurt will thicken.

Yoghurt Cheese

It is also simple to make your own yoghurt cheese. Use a double thickness of muslin to line a colander, pour in the yoghurt, secure the four corners of the muslin with string and tie this up so that the whey drips into a bowl. After several hours you will have creamy thick curds in the muslin. The longer you let the whey drip out the thicker the curds. For a *Greek* yoghurt consistency 2 hours is enough. For making cheesecake let it hang overnight. 575ml (1 pint) yoghurt will make 225g (8 oz) thick yoghurt cheese.

Greek yoghurt is made with either ewe's, cow's or goat's milk. It is thick because much of the whey has been extracted (see yoghurt cheese above).

Quark

This is a low fat soft cheese which is now widely available in delicatessens, health stores and some supermarkets. It is very similar to Paneer (Indian lemon cheese) and made either with milk or skimmed milk and curdled with fresh lemon juice.

To make quark, simply bring 1.1 litre (2 pints) milk to boil, remove the pan from the heat and stir in 4 tablespoons of fresh lemon juice. Leave to stand for 10 minutes then bring the mixture to boil again and take it immediately off the heat. Line a large colander with a double thickness of muslin, pour in the curdled mixture and let most of the whey run through the cloth. Tie the edges of the cloth with string and let the whey drip through for 1½ hours (do not squeeze). Scrape off the curds and chill before using. Keeps for only 2 to 3 days in the refrigerator.

Fromage Blanc

A low fat soft cheese which was traditionally made with single cream or full fat milk, but is now commercially made with skimmed milk. It is similar to quark but instead of lemon juice, rennet is used as a curdling agent. For those who do not wish to use animal rennet it can be made quite easily as you can now buy vegetable rennet.

Heat 1.1 litre (2 pints) milk to 50°c (110°F). Remove from heat and stir in 4 to 5 drops rennet. Allow to stand covered for 24 hours at an average temperature of 30°c (60°F). When set, line a colander with muslin, pour in the set mixture, tie up the edges of the muslin, suspend and leave to drip for 1 hour. Scrape off the soft curds and chill before using. Keeps for only 2 to 3 days in the refrigerator.

Soya Milk

This is widely available but expensive. However, it is not difficult and very cheap to make. It freezes well.

Wash the beans and pick over for small stones. Soak for 24 hours changing the water at least 3 times during soaking. Rinse and liquidize the beans 1 cup at a time to 1 cup of boiling water. Leave the motor on for 1½ minutes each batch. Lightly oil a large 5 litre (10 pint) capacity saucepan, pour in 8 cups of fresh water, bring to boil and pour in the liquidized bean purée. Bring to boil stirring constantly. Turn down to low and simmer for 20 minutes. The mixture will be frothy so to check if it is simmering, spoon back some of the froth and see if it is gently rolling and bubbling underneath. Stir occasionally. Put a double thickness of muslin over a colander snuggly fitted into a large clean pot or bowl to catch the milk. Pour in the bean liquid. Put on rubber gloves, pull the edge of the muslin together and twist and prod to get as much milk out as possible. Open muslin and pour in 4 200ml (8 fl oz) tea cups of boiling water, then twist and prod again. The soya milk is now ready.

If freezing, cool the soya milk quickly by immersing the bowl in cold water, changing the water as it warms. Keeps fresh for 4 days in the 'fridge and 3 months if frozen. (To make soya milk yoghurt see Yoghurt, page 15).

Tofu

A soya bean curd cheese which is widely available in health stores and Chinese grocers. It is made from soya milk which is curdled with a solution of nigari crystals and water. Nigari is the residue left after salt (sodium chloride) and water are removed from sea water.

Tofu is a complete protein food (see Pulses, pages 19–20), rich in minerals and a good supply of B and E vitamins. It is also cholesterol-free and very low in calories. Most protein-rich foods have an acid effect on the body but tofu has an alkaline effect. It is great for slimmers and deserves experimenting with. You will find that I have used it extensively throughout the book in the vegan menus.

If you wish to make it, see my book 'Making Your Own Home Proteins' for explicit details. From just 350g (12 oz) dry weight soya beans you will get 450g (1 lb) firm tofu. Firm tofu has all the whey extracted whereas silken tofu contains all the curds and whey, is wobbly, and best for some desserts and salad dressings.

Coconut Milk

You can buy a very good quality coconut milk in cans and it is quite delicious in curry sauces (see Pumpkin Molee Curry page 70). However, it is simple to make thick or thin using freshly grated coconut or desiccated. For best results soak the coconut in the water overnight.

To 225g (8 oz) freshly grated or desiccated coconut add 900ml (1½ pints) boiling water. Cover and leave to stand overnight. Liquidize this mixture then strain through a muslin-lined colander squeezing out as much moisture as possible. This is called thick coconut milk. For thin milk, pour 575ml (1 pint) hot water over the pulp left in the muslin. Leave for 1 hour and then strain through the muslin as you did for thick milk. It freezes very well.

Pasta

Wholewheat pasta in all shapes and sizes is widely available. It is very easy to make, especially if you have a pasta machine. What is important is the consistency of the dough, letting the dough rest before rolling out and, if cutting into ribbons for tagliatelle, drying the ribboned noodles by hanging them from a bar for a few hours or placing them between 2 lightly floured cloths. There is no need to dry canelloni or lasagne shapes. You can make a rich wholemeal egg pasta dough or, for vegans, a simple dough from wholemeal flour and water. You can also make the dough green (pasta verdi) by adding spinach or light red by adding tomato purée, see below.

Egg Pasta Dough
_____ Makes approximately 450g (1 lb) _____

450g (1 lb) strong wholemeal flour
4 large eggs
1 very level tsp sea salt
1 tbsp cold-pressed olive or sunflower oil
4 tbsps cold water

Sift the flour and salt into a large mixing bowl. Make a well and pour in unbeaten eggs, oil and water. Gradually incorporate the flour into the liquids and work well together to form a stiffish dough. You may need a little more water but don't make the dough sticky. Knead for 12 minutes until you have a smooth and elastic dough. Let the dough rest by placing in a polythene bag. Put a cloth on top of the opening but leave space around the dough in the bag. Your basic dough is now ready to use either in a pasta machine or for rolling out and cutting into the shapes you require for individual recipes.

Eggless Pasta Dough

450g (1 lb) strong wholemeal
    flour
1 tsp sea salt

4 tbsps cold-pressed olive or
    sunflower oil
8 tbsps cold water

Use method as for Egg Pasta Dough above, do not make the dough
sticky as it must be fairly stiff before kneading.

Green Pasta (Pasta Verdi)

If using spinach you will need fewer eggs in the ingredients
and the water will have to be judged by you. It depends on
how much water you leave in the cooked spinach.

450g (1 lb) strong wholemeal
    flour
1 level tsp sea salt
450g (1 lb) spinach, lightly
    cooked

2 large eggs
1 tbsp cold-pressed olive or
    sunflower oil
cold water if necessary

Sift the flour and salt into a bowl. Drain spinach a little (leave some of
the water in it), liquidize until smooth. Put this with the eggs and oil into
a well in the centre of the flour. Follow by mixing, kneading and
resting, as for Egg Pasta Dough (page 18), adding a little cold water if
necessary.

Light Red Pasta

Instead of 4 tablespoons of water in the Egg Pasta Dough (page 18),
use 1 tablespoon cold water and 3 rounded tablespoons tomato
purée. Follow by mixing, kneading and resting the dough as for Egg
Pasta Dough.

The green and the light red pasta can both be made without eggs for
vegans. Adjust the water to form the firmish dough.

All homemade pasta cooks quicker than bought pasta. Boil in
plenty of lightly salted water for 6 to 8 minutes maximum.

Pulses

These are dried peas, beans and lentils. Their protein content ranges from 17% to 25% with the exception of the soya bean which is approximately 40% protein. They are a good source of vitamins and minerals and are high in fibre. Except for the soya bean, pulses are not complete protein foods. A complete protein food is one that contains all the amino acids which the body needs to build protein. There are approximately 20 known amino acids making up human protein. The body produces 14 and the other 8, which are known as essential amino acids, must be obtained from the diet. Meat, fish, dairy produce and the soya bean contain these essential acids. Combining pulses with other foods which contain the missing proteins will produce a complete protein food with all the amino acids in balance. The complementary foods are whole grains, nuts and seeds, and dairy produce. Proper soaking and cooking of pulses is vital because they all contain adverse substances which, in their raw state only, are harmful to the digestion. The recipes in the book where pulses are used will give you the correct method of cooking to destroy these harmful inhibitors.

Whole Grains or Cereals
These contain, in their whole state, good amounts of protein, are high in fibre and rich in minerals and vitamins. Processed grains contain no fibre, have very little nutritional value and are mainly starch. All whole grain cereals and flours have a shorter shelf life than processed grains because they contain the valuable germ oil. Use all whole grain flours within 2 months. Store in airtight containers in a cool place away from light. Whole berries or grains such as wholewheat berries, brown rice and pot barley (pearl barley is polished and processed) will keep for 1 year if stored in the same way and millet will keep up to 2 years in similar conditions. Whole grains have much more flavour than processed grains and once you learn how to cook these to perfection, processed devitalized grains will seem very insipid by comparison.

The recipes in the book give full instructions on how to cook whole grains where listed as an ingredient. You will find that I have used unbleached white flour and 81% wheatmeal flour occasionally, the former for sauces and the latter for light bread and pastry, but if your diet is basically a healthy one and rich in high fibre foods, using processed foods occasionally can't really do much harm.

Fibre
Fibre which is the structural part of plants, plays a vital role in eliminating waste products from the body. Without going into too many technical details a lack of fibre can, at the very least, cause

constipation which if prolonged may cause a very painful disease called diverticulitis, making elimination impossible and surgery inevitable. Much evidence points to a strong connection between a low fibre diet and cancer of the colon. Diverticulitis is present in approximately 10% of all men and women in this country over the age of 40.

Fibre can also alter bacteria in the bowel making it less prone to disease. No you don't have to eat that awful sawdust-like product bran, you will get plenty of fibre in a well balanced diet which includes the following foods: whole grains, pulses, nuts and seeds, fresh fruit and vegetables. Meat, fish and dairy produce contain no fibre so it is essential to balance these foods with those high in fibre.

Nuts
Nuts are a high protein food rich in the B vitamins and, although they have quite a high fat content, they are rich in linoleic acid which helps control the levels of cholesterol in the blood (see Oils page 14). Avoid commercially packed salted nuts as these often contain artificial additives and are sometimes roasted in saturated fats.

Seeds
Seeds are a good source of protein, are jam-packed with vitamins and minerals and contain a good supply of linoleic acid (see Oils, page 14). Pumpkin seeds, sunflower seeds and sesame seeds are used throughout the book. Try them on your breakfast cereals, in biscuits and lightly toasted with a little shoyu (soya sauce) for a healthy nibble. Sunflower seeds are best for this. Simply spread some seeds on a non-stick baking sheet. Sprinkle on a few drops of shoyu, rub this in with your fingers and bake at 160°c/325°F/Gas Mark 3 for 12 minutes. Leave to get cold and crisp on the tray. Keep in a screw-top jar. Children love these.

Meat and Poultry
Meat and poultry are complete protein foods (see Pulses pages 19–20). They are rich in vitamins and minerals, have no fibre and contain large amounts of saturated fats which are known to increase the level of cholesterol in the blood and thus make us more prone to heart attacks. Added to this, animals reared for meat production are often injected with growth promoters, hormones and antibiotics, the residue of which are found in the meat we eat. Naturally reared animals produce leaner meat which has a far better flavour and is free from substances which are now considered harmful to our health. Ideally

the free-range meat would seem to be the wisest choice to try to obtain. Keep asking and seek out suppliers of naturally produced meat. To help cut down on the saturated fats, trim all meat of fat, or better still, buy lean cuts. Skin poultry if jointing it and mince your own lean meat. Bought mince is often very fatty.

In the Meat Lovers Menus I have used far less meat in the recipes than is traditionally eaten but combined with the other foods in the menu, I think you will have very satisfying and flavoursome meals.

Fish

Fish is a complete protein food (see Pulses page 19–20). White fish contains hardly any fat, what fat there is is unsaturated (see Oils page 14). The unsaturated fat in oily fish such as mackerel and herrings helps lower the level of cholesterol in the blood and these two varieties are particularly rich in vitamin D. Freshly caught free-range fish has much more flavour then fish reared on fish farms. But sadly, pollution in the waters is badly contaminating and often killing this nutritionally valuable food so I think we have to fight to keep our waters free of pollution if we want to eat healthy fish.

Eggs

Most of the eggs consumed in this country and abroad are battery eggs which, research has revealed, often contain residues of antibiotics, hormones and other drugs fed to the hens. These residues are now proving to have adverse effects on humans. Free-range eggs are the product of healthy, naturally fed hens who have adequate space to scratch about and exercise in the open air. There is some controversy as to whether eggs, because of their high cholesterol content, contribute to heart disease. Eggs also contain lecithin which breaks fats into tiny globules easily. This process helps the body to utilize cholesterol normally. The lecithin content in eggs is considered enough to protect against high levels of cholesterol in the body. You can buy free-range eggs in health stores and in some supermarkets. Keep asking for them and use only 3 to 4 eggs per week per person and there might just be enough of the free-range variety to go around.

Seaweeds

These much neglected highly nutritious sea vegetables are well worth getting to know. They are rich in vitamins, minerals and trace elements.

Arame and Hiziki which are string-like, are delicious with stir-fry vegetables and rice dishes. 25 g (1 oz) of either, soaked in cold wate for 15 minutes, squeezed then fried with the vegetables, is enough to add to approximately 225g (8 oz) dry weight rice with complementary vegetables.

Dulse or Dillisk is superb washed and chopped then added to salad vegetables.

Kombu is used in Japan as the basis of dashi (basic stock) and soups. Wakame also adds a nutritious and delicate flavour to soups and stews.

Agar-agar

Agar-agar is a product of strong-tasting red seaweeds and is sold in either powdered or flake form. If you are on a vegetarian or vegan diet, agar-agar is the perfect alternative to gelatine which is animal based. Use about 1 rounded teaspoon of the powder or flakes to 275ml (½ pint) of liquid for a good firm jelly. It will not set in the presence of acetic or oxalic acid which is found in wine, vinegar, chocolate, spinach and tomatoes.

Condiments

These all contain salt and should be used sparingly.

Salt

It is now fully accepted that a high salt (sodium) intake can seriously damage our health. It can cause fluid retention which in turn can result in excessive weight gain. We need less than 1g, about ½ a teaspoon, daily but 10 times this amount is often consumed.

Sea salt has a slightly lower sodium content but the level is still high and all salt should be used with caution.

Gomacio

This is a delicious condiment and is great sprinkled on omelettes, poached or boiled eggs, and vegetable and rice dishes.
To make Gomacio:
To 20 parts sesame seeds, you will need 1 part sea salt. Toast the seeds in a dry, heavy-based pan on moderate heat until a deep golden brown and popping. Grind with the salt in a liquidizer until powdery in texture. Stored in a screw-top jar, this will keep for several weeks.

Vegetable Bouillon Powder

There are several brands of this on the market. It is simply dried and powdered herbs, spices and salt – a powdered vegetable stock cube mixture. It is delicious in soups and stews and in salad dressings instead of salt. Herb salt is very similar and can be used in the same way.

Shoyu
Shoyu is a naturally fermented soya sauce, free from artificial colours and flavourings. It is a live food produced from soya beans brewed over a period of 18 months with roasted wheat and sea salt. This process produces a source of vitamin B12 (see page 17). When added to foods such as whole grains, pulses, nuts and seeds, it increases the amount of protein that can be digested. It should be added after cooking as heat destroys the live enzymes which aid digestion.

Tamari
This is slightly thicker and stronger than shoyu and is produced without the wheat, so for those on a gluten-free diet it is ideal.

Sugar and Fruit Sugar
Like salt, sugar (sucrose) is another food which should be used with discretion. Why is it so bad for us? It is the major source of tooth decay. Excessive use causes obesity, and is a contributing factor in cases of heart disease and diabetes. Most jams (unless they state no sugar) contain 60% sugar, many chutneys 50% and many bought cakes and biscuits not only have a high sugar content but are also high in saturated fats (see Oils page 14).

Fruit sugar- (fructose-) based concentrates which include honey, pure maple syrup, fruit juice concentrates and the product manufactured from fruit which looks like caster sugar have also to be used in moderation. However, fruit sugar (fructose) is absorbed more slowly from the intestinal tract than ordinary sugar (sucrose) and therefore does not cause the blood sugar to rise sharply. Although I have used a little sugar in the recipes you will mostly find fruit sugar-based products are used to sweeten wherever possible.

Carob
Carob powder or flour is a naturally sweet chocolate-like flavoured product of the locust bean. Unlike chocolate it is caffeine-free and lower in fat than cocoa. For those of you who are allergic to chocolate it is a marvellous alternative. It is very cheap and can be used in most recipes where cocoa is an ingredient.

About the Menus

You will find that you can adapt all the menus in the book to suit your taste and that each menu remains balanced nutritionally. You will also find that in all three diets catered for, you can prepare irresistible meals which are healthy and not too expensive.

As the menus evolved I was amazed how little the variation for the different diets needed changing, so those of you who have a vegetarian or vegan in the family or who happen to be entertaining vegetarians or vegans, will see how easy it is to incorporate dishes in each menu and please everyone.

This year I prepared a wedding feast for my son. Most of the 80 guests were meat eaters and many had not tasted brown rice, not to mention a nut roast. I did the Summer Celebration Menu (page 86) plus the Turkey and Vegetable Terrine in the Meat Lovers Menu (page 111). All the food was quickly consumed with obvious delight and pleasure, after 2 hours only a little cheese remained.

Throughout the menus, other than those which cater for large parties, some of the portions might seem smaller than you are used to providing for a particular number of guests, but it is the whole menu combined which makes a complete meal so there is no need for large portions of any individual dish.

Bon appetit!

Menus Just for Two

When I first started cooking seriously at the age of 16 I was so eager to show off my 'culinary genius' that staging a dinner party for two never really occured to me. Now, having brought up four children, catered for their likes and dislikes, feasted their friends and mine over many years and more recently run my own natural food shop and small restaurant, it is a sheer delight to prepare a special meal for one treasured friend and myself.

Just imagine the table set – flowers in the centre, candles ready to light; the wine, if white, chilling and your favourite music playing. This is the perfect setting to experiment with unfamiliar foods, especially if you are new to a more natural way of eating and, for those who are real beginners in the art of cooking, there are only two of you to eat any disasters. Hopefully, you will have no such disasters with the following four menus which I trust will delight your palate and stimulate you to spoil yourself in the future with many more dinner parties for two.

These menus can quite easily be doubled or trebled to serve 4 to 6. So when you find a real winner, preparing a tried and tested menu for larger numbers will obviously cause less anxiety than tackling completely new dishes for those more elaborate occasions.

The first menu is one I am looking forward to enjoying this very evening. After preparing my young daughter's birthday party yesterday I think I deserve it.

Spring Menu

❁ VEGETARIAN ❁

Chick Pea, Watercress and Mint Soup
Green Vegetable Strudel with
Red Pepper Sauce
Lettuce, Alfalfa, Primrose & Violet Salad with
Chive Vinaigrette
Spiced Mango & Yoghurt Ice
Sesame & Ginger Snaps (page 137)

Chick Pea, Watercress and Mint Soup

This is a refreshing and delicious Middle Eastern-style soup and is best served with either Garlic French Loaf or Nutritious Baguettes (page 106). The ingredients here are just for two generous servings but it's worth trebling the recipe and freezing what you do not need. The soup makes a quick and nourishing lunch dish if served with garlic bread and cheese.

110g (4 oz) chick peas, dry weight
little sea salt
1 tbsp cold-pressed sunflower or olive oil
1 good size leek, trimmed and sliced
1 large clove garlic, peeled and crushed
1 very level tsp coriander seeds, ground

1 tbsp fresh parsley, chopped
1 level tbsp fresh mint, chopped or 1 level tsp dried
1 tbsp lemon juice
1 dessertspoon vegetable bouillon powder
1 small bunch watercress, finely chopped
freshly ground black pepper to taste
few watercress leaves to garnish

Soak the chick peas overnight, changing the water 3 times. Drain, rinse and add 900ml (1½ pints) cold water. Bring to boil, boil for 10 minutes, turn down to simmer and cook for about 45 minutes until the chick peas are soft. Drain, measure the liquid and reserve 575ml (1 pint). Heat the oil in a heavy-based saucepan and fry the leeks, garlic and coriander seeds for 2 minutes. Add parsley, mint, lemon juice, vegetable bouillon powder, 575ml (1 pint) chick pea cooking liquid and the chick peas. Bring to boil, turn down to simmer and cook for 6 minutes. Add the watercress and cook for a further 5 minutes. Liquidize and return to the saucepan. Season with freshly ground black pepper.

When ready to serve reheat, pour into a serving bowl and garnish with a twist of black pepper and watercress leaves.

Green Vegetable Strudel

Strudel or filo pastry is very tricky and time consuming to make so I suggest you buy the pastry which is frozen and quite simple to use.
The fillings for strudels, both savoury and sweet, are endless. What is important is that the filling must not be too wet or the pastry will tear. The size required in the recipe is the size you buy. Always make the filling before you prepare the strudel or filo sheets.
You can use 50g (2 oz) of wholemeal breadcrumbs instead of the almonds.

FILLING

50g (2 oz) blanched almonds
175g (6 oz) goat's curd or
   ricotta cheese
½ medium size avocado
   peeled, stoned and chopped
1 tbsp lemon juice
1 large egg yolk
¼ level tsp ground mace
1 tbsp fresh parsley, chopped
1 level tsp dried tarragon
1 rounded tsp vegetable
   bouillon powder
freshly ground black pepper
1 tbsp cold-pressed sunflower
   oil

110g (4 oz) broccoli spears,
   steamed for 5 mins. and
   chopped
110g (4 oz) leeks, cut in thin
   rings (weight when trimmed)
2 small courgettes, cut in
   1.25cm (½ in) thin sticks
50g (2 oz) small button
   mushrooms, sliced
1 rounded tsp gram flour (chick
   pea flour)

STRUDEL (FILO) CRUST

4 sheets of strudel (filo) pastry,
   50 × 30cm (20 × 12 in)
little lukewarm cold-pressed oil
few sesame seeds to top

For the filling:
Lightly toast the blanched almonds in the oven, 160°c/325°F/Gas Mark 3, for about 15 minutes. Meanwhile, heat the oil in a medium size non-stick frying pan. Sauté the leeks and courgettes on moderate heat stirring constantly for about 3 minutes. Stir in the mushrooms and continue to fry for a further 2 minutes. Take off heat and spoon onto a plate to cool slightly. Grind the almonds to a medium crumb texture. Be careful not to make them too powdery.

Put cheese, chopped avocado, lemon juice, egg yolk, mace, parsley, tarragon, vegetable bouillon powder, gram flour and a little freshly ground black pepper into a food processor or blender until smooth. Scoop out into a mixing bowl. Stir in the broccoli, sautéed vegetables and ground almonds.

For the strudel (filo) crust
Preheat oven, 190°c/375°F/Gas Mark 5. Defrost the pastry and carefully peel off 4 sheets. Place a large damp piece of muslin or thin cotton on a work surface. Lay 1 sheet of pastry on this and brush with the lukewarm oil. Top with the other sheets brushing each one with oil as you do so. (Don't worry if the pastry tears a little, just stick it together.) Spoon the filling on to one of the narrow ends of the rectangle 5cm (2 in) from the top edge and 4cm (1½ in) from either side. Fold first the two long edges over the filling and then the far end. Lift the thin cloth up gently and roll up the pastry. Oil a baking sheet and ease the strudel roll off the cloth and on to the baking sheet. Seal end down. Brush top with a little oil and sprinkle on the sesame seeds. Bake in the preheated oven for 30 minutes.

Place on a warmed serving dish and serve with the Red Pepper Sauce in a separate bowl.
Note: If you have a little too much filling then make a small strudel by using just 1 sheet of strudel or filo pastry. Oil in the same way, fold it in half, spoon the leftover filling in and fold and top in the same way.

Cook with the larger strudel keeping them apart and when cold feeze for a little lunch for one. To heat, simply defrost and heat in a moderate oven for 10 to 15 minutes.

Red Pepper Sauce

1 medium to large size red
   pepper
1 tbsp cold-pressed sunflower
   or olive oil
1 small onion, very finely
   chopped
1 clove garlic, crushed
1 large ripe tomato or 2 canned
   tomatoes

small sprig fresh lemon thyme
   or ½ level tsp dried
3 large fresh basil leaves or ½
   level tsp dried
½ bay leaf
4 tbsp dry white wine
¼ level tsp fruit sugar
little sea salt and freshly ground
   black pepper

Grill the pepper on maximum heat for 5 minutes, turning to brown on all sides. Turn down heat to moderate and continue to toast the pepper turning constantly until the skin is blistered and charred all over. Pop into a colander and rinse in cold water as you rub the skin off. Pat dry, cut in half, remove seeds and pith, and chop. Blanch tomato in boiling water for 3 minutes. Skin and press through a fine sieve (if canned then press through an ordinary sieve). Heat the oil in a small non-stick pan. Sweat the onion and garlic for 1 minute on a low heat with the lid on. Take off lid and turn heat up. Just as the onion is beginning to go golden stir in the chopped peppers, herbs, sieved tomato pulp, white wine (or water), fruit sugar, sea salt and freshly ground black pepper to your taste. Stir well together. Turn heat to low, replace lid and cook on gentle heat for 10 minutes. Take out thyme sprig and bay leaf and liquidize until smooth.

Lettuce, Alfalfa, Primrose & Violet Salad with Chive Vinaigrette

If you can't obtain the wild flowers easily then simply use small rose petals.

1 small lettuce with a good heart
50g (2 oz) sprouted weight alfalfa (see page 12 on sprouting)
few primroses and violets, stems removed, or rose petals
CHIVE VINAIGRETTE
3 tbsps cold-pressed sunflower or olive oil
1 tbsp lemon juice
1 level tsp vegetable bouillon powder
freshly ground black pepper
pinch fruit sugar or a few drops of clear honey
2 tbsps chopped chives

Wash lettuce well. Shake off water and keep leaves whole. Arrange on a flattish plate putting the greener leaves around the edge of the dish and the lighter leaves in the centre. Sprinkle with the sprouted alfalfa.

Put all the vinaigrette ingredients in a blender and process until smooth and green. When ready to serve pour this over the salad.

Arrange the flowers on top placing the violets on the lighter lettuce leaves and the primroses around the edge on the darker leaves.

Spiced Mango & Yoghurt Ice

Dried mangos when hydrated taste amazingly like fresh ones and are much cheaper and easier to prepare. They need 8 hours soaking to obtain full flavour.

50g (2 oz) dried mango
225ml (8 fl oz) apple juice
½ cinnamon stick
¼ level tsp freshly ground
 allspice or nutmeg
1 level tsp fresh ginger root,
 grated
large sprig of mint

2 tsps Kirsch (optional but
 delicious)
225g (8 oz) carton Greek
 strained yoghurt
1 large egg, separated
25g (1 oz) fruit sugar
little ground cinnamon and fresh
 mint leaves to garnish

In a small piece of muslin put the broken up cinnamon stick, the ground allspice and the grated ginger. Tie up into a little purse. Wash the dried mango and drain. Put apple juice and muslin purse into a saucepan. Bring to boil and pour over the mango, pushing the purse down into the centre of the liquid and fruit. Press in the sprig of mint. Cover and let stand for 8 hours stirring from time to time. Take out 3 tablespoons of the soaking liquid and reserve. Purée the mango with the rest of the soaking liquid until smooth.

In a liquidizer, blend the egg yolk with the sugar until very creamy. Bring the reserved 3 tablespoons of soaking liquid and sugar to boil and cook on gentle heat until bubbles flatten. Now pour the hot syrup into the beaten egg mixture with liquidizer on full speed. Keep blending until mixture is thick and cold. Stir yoghurt into mango purée, then stir in the creamed egg yolk. Whisk egg white in a small bowl until stiff and fold into the mango mixture. Freeze in a plastic container with a lid on for 3 hours. Whisk twice during freezing time, about every 50 minutes.

Allow to thaw in the main part of the 'fridge for 30 minutes before serving. Spoon into individual serving bowls, sprinkle on a little ground cinnamon and plant a sprig of mint in the centre of each portion. Serve with sesame and ginger snaps (see page 137 for recipe).

Spring Menu for Vegans

In the recipe for Green Vegetable Strudel (page 29) leave out the goat's curd cheese and add 175g (6 oz) firm tofu. Omit the egg yolk, the mixture will bind well enough without it. Prepare and cook in the same way as in the vegetarian recipe.

In the recipe for Spiced Mango & Yoghurt Ice (page 33) do the following recipe for:

Spiced Mango and Tofu Ice

Follow instructions for preparing the dried mango purée, then blend the soaking juices with 225g (8 oz) silken tofu and 25g (1 oz) of fruit sugar. Stir in the mango purée and freeze in the same way as in the vegetarian recipe. The result will be more like a sorbet but still delicious.

Spring Menu for Meat Lovers

Instead of the recipe for Green Vegetable Strudel (page 29) do:

Green Vegetable and Ham Strudel

FILLING:

225g (8 oz) lean green bacon, slices (weight when fat removed)
1 tbsp cold-pressed sunflower oil
110g (4 oz) leeks, cut in thin rings (weight when trimmed)
2 small courgettes, cut in 1cm (½ in) slices
50g (2 oz) small button mushrooms, sliced
110g (4 oz) broccoli spears, chopped
1 tbsp fresh parsley, chopped
1 level tsp dried tarragon
½ medium size cooking apple, peeled, cored and minced
1 large egg yolk
1 tbsp Greek plain yoghurt
50g (2 oz) wholemeal breadcrumbs
freshly ground black pepper

Fry the lean meat in the oil for 3 minutes and then mince. Sauté the leeks and courgettes in the same oil on moderate heat for 3 minutes. Add the mushrooms and continue to fry for 2 minutes more. Spoon into a mixing bowl and stir in the other ingredients.

Prepare the pastry, fill, roll up, brush top and bake.

Serve with the Red Pepper Sauce (page 31) as in the vegetarian menu.

The rest of the menu remains the same.

❀   VEGETARIAN   ❀

Avocado, Peach & Mushroom Salad with
Tofu & Herb Mayonnaise
Stuffed Marrow in Piquant Tomato Sauce
Simple Savoury Rice
Broccoli Florets with Baby Carrots
Summer Fruit Compote with Raspberry Sauce

——————————— ———————————

Avocado, Peach & Mushroom Salad with Tofu & Herb Mayonnaise

1 medium size avocado, skinned, cut in half and stoned
little lemon juice
1 peach, blanched for 1 min. in boiling water, cut in half, stoned and peeled
50g (2 oz) small button mushrooms
few leaves of curly endive, washed and patted dry
TOFU HERB MAYONNAISE
150g (5 oz) silken tofu
1 tbsp lemon juice
1 tbsp cold-pressed olive or sunflower oil

1 very small clove garlic, crushed
1 level tbsp finely chopped parsley
1 level tbsp finely chopped fresh basil or marjoram or level tsp dried
sprinkling of vegetable bouillon powder
¼ tsp Dijon mustard
freshly ground black pepper
few sprigs of basil or marjoram to garnish if using fresh herbs

Cut off 4 thin slices of avocado for garnish and chop the rest into small chunks. Sprinkle on some lemon juice to stop the avocado browning. Cut off 4 thin slices of peach and chop the rest into small chunks. Wash and wipe the mushrooms and cut in thin slices. Arrange a bed of curly endive in the bottom of 2 individual shallow serving bowls. Mix the chopped avocado, peach and mushrooms together in a mixing bowl. Put all the tofu herb mayonnaise ingredients, except the black pepper, in a blender and process until smooth. Add black pepper to your taste. Add more vegetable bouillon powder if you wish. Fork this into the avocado mixture and then spoon on to the endive beds.

Garnish with the avocado and peach slices and a sprig of fresh basil or marjoram if using. Chill until ready to serve.

Stuffed Marrow in Piquant Tomato Sauce

If you are fortunate enough to grow your own vegetables and have an overgrown courgette, especially the more tender golden variety, you can use this instead of a marrow. You will need a deep oval flameproof casserole dish with a lid.

1 900g (2 lb) marrow

STUFFING

2 tbsp cold-pressed sunflower oil

1 medium size onion, finely chopped

2 level tbsps fresh parsley, chopped

75g (3 oz) medium finely ground almonds

50g (2 oz) medium finely ground cashew nuts

60g (2½ oz) wholemeal breadcrumbs

1 tsp vegetable bouillon powder

1 small egg

PIQUANT TOMATO SAUCE

2 tbsps olive or cold-pressed sunflower oil

1 medium size onion, chopped

1 tender stick celery (use green leaf end)

1 large clove garlic, crushed

1 small red pepper, finely chopped

1 rounded tsp coriander seeds, ground

½ level tsp cayenne pepper

1 bay leaf

1 level tbsp fresh basil, chopped or 1 tsp dried

½ tsp dried oregano

225g (8 oz) either fresh, ripe tomatoes, skinned and chopped or use canned, chopped

½ tsp vegetable bouillon powder

freshly ground black pepper

1 tbsp lemon juice

4 tbsps freshly grated Parmesan or Cheddar cheese

pinch dried oregano

Trim stalk off marrow. Cut in half lengthwise and scoop out seeds. Bring half a large saucepan of water to boil and cook the marrow for 10 minutes. Drain well on a wire rack, skin side up, while you make the filling and sauce.

For the stuffing:
Heat oil in a large frying pan. Sauté the onion for 5 minutes on low heat with the lid on. Put parsley, nuts, breadcrumbs, bouillon powder and egg in a mixing bowl. Stir in the sautéed onion and bind well together.

To make the sauce:
Heat oil in a large frying pan. Sauté the onion, garlic and celery for 7 minutes until soft. Add the red pepper, coriander, cayenne pepper, bay leaf, basil and oregano and fry for 3 minutes more. Stir in the tomatoes, vegetable bouillon powder, black pepper, and lemon juice. Cook on gentle heat until the sauce thickens. Take out the bay leaf and liquidize.

Put the drained marrow halves in a greased oval or rectangular casserole dish. Divide the filling and stuff this into the hollow of the marrow. Spoon over the tomato sauce and sprinkle on the cheese and a little dried oregano. Bake for approximately 25 minutes on 190°c/375°F/Gas Mark 5, until the cheese is golden brown on top.

Simple Savoury Rice

150g (5 oz) Italian long grain
   brown rice
1 medium size onion, peeled
   and finely chopped
1 tbsp cold-pressed sunflower
   oil

275ml (½ pint) hot water
2 level tsps vegetable bouillon
   powder
few sprigs of flat-leafed parsley
   to garnish

Wash the rice by putting in a sieve and letting cold water run through the grains for 1 minute. Drain well. Heat oil in a medium size heavy-based saucepan. Sauté the onion for about 7 minutes on moderate heat until slightly browned. Stir in the rice grains and continue to fry for 3 minutes. Pour in the hot water and vegetable bouillon powder. Bring to boil, turn down to simmer and cook with a tight lid on for 35 minutes. Do not stir the rice. When cooked the water will all be absorbed and the grains separate. Place in a warm serving bowl and garnish with the parsley sprigs.

Broccoli Florets with Baby Carrots

225g (8 oz) broccoli spears, washed
12 baby carrots, scrubbed

1 tsp cold-pressed sunflower oil
1 tsp lemon juice
pinch sea salt

Steam broccoli for 5 minutes. Steam whole baby carrots for 10 minutes or until cooked but still firm.

To arrange in a serving dish cut stems off the broccoli, chop these and put in the centre of the dish. Put broccoli florets on top and the whole carrots around the edge. Mix the oil, lemon juice and pinch of sea salt together and sprinkle over the top.

Summer Fruit Compote with Raspberry Sauce

1 tsp finely grated orange and lemon rind, mixed
good pinch ground cinnamon
tiny pinch clove powder
4 tbsps apple juice concentrate
2 tbsps water
75g (3 oz) red currants

75g (3 oz) black currants
75g (3 oz) strawberries, cut in half lengthwise
1 large banana, cut in slanting ovals
110g (4 oz) raspberries
1 tbsp Cointreau (optional)

Put lemon rind, cinnamon, clove, apple juice concentrate and water into a heavy-based non-stick saucepan. Heat slowly then add the red currants, black currants, strawberries and banana slices. Cook on very low heat for 3 minutes. Remove from heat and take fruit out with a slotted spoon. Place in a serving dish. Sieve the raspberries into a bowl. Add the cooking juices and stir in the Cointreau if using. Pour this over the poached fruit and chill well before serving.

This is delicious and refreshing alone or served with Yoghurt Cream (page 102).

Summer Menu for Vegans

In the recipe for Stuffed Marrow in Piquant Tomato Sauce omit the egg from the stuffing and add 1 dessertspoon buckwheat flour mixed with a little water to bind the nut mixture. Omit the cheese and instead use thin slices of firm tofu spread on top.

The rest of the menu remains the same.

Summer Menu for Meat Lovers

In the recipe for Stuffed Marrow in Piquant Tomato Sauce you can easily substitute 225g (8 oz) minced, raw chicken, lamb, ham, or beef for the nuts in the stuffing. Fry the onion as in the vegetarian version then add the minced meat and continue to fry for a further 10 minutes. Mix with the other stuffing ingredients and continue as directed in the vegetarian menu.

The rest of the menu remains the same.

❃ VEGETARIAN ❃

Pumpkin & Aniseed Soup

Chick Pea Bake

Juniper Sauce

Yoghurt Cream Potatoes

Brussels Sprouts with Carrots

Cinnamon Apple Slices with Blackberry Sauce

———— ————

Pumpkin & Aniseed Soup

350g (12 oz) pumpkin, diced
1 clove garlic, crushed
½ tsp aniseed
200ml (7 fl oz) boiling water
1 tbsp cold-pressed safflower oil
170g (6 oz) fresh tomatoes,
   skinned and chopped

1 dessertspoon fresh parsley,
   chopped
sea salt and freshly ground
   black pepper
little chopped parsley to garnish
2 star anise to garnish (optional)

Sauté the pumpkin, garlic and aniseed for 3 minutes. Add all the other ingredients except the salt and pepper. Bring to boil, turn down heat and simmer with the lid on for 20 minutes. Cool and liquidize. Taste and add a little sea salt and freshly ground black pepper. Reheat when ready to serve and sprinkle on a little chopped parsley and the star anise if using.

Chick Pea Bake

You will have enough of this bake to serve cold with salad for a light lunch for two the following day. Soaking and cooking dried peas and beans can be a bother so why not get two meals for two out of this tasty bake.

225g (8 oz) chick peas, dry weight
50g (2 oz) porridge oats
1 large Spanish onion, finely chopped
1 large juicy clove garlic, crushed
2 tbsps cold-pressed sunflower oil
1 small green pepper, deseeded and finely chopped
2 tbsps fresh parsley, chopped
1 small sprig fresh mint, chopped
1 rounded tsp coriander seeds, ground

1 level tsp cumin seeds
½ level tsp cayenne pepper (optional)
2 tbsps lemon juice
2 level tbsps sunflower seed spread
1 large egg
freshly ground black pepper and sea salt to taste
little oil for top
½ cucumber, sliced, for garnish
½ lemon, sliced, for garnish

For the Chick Pea Bake:
Soak the chick peas for 12 hours changing the water at least 3 times during soaking. Rinse and cook the peas in fresh water for 1 hour or until soft. Drain and mince the chick peas. Sauté the onion and garlic in the oil for 5 minutes then stir in the minced chick peas. Add all other ingredients except the oil for basting. Oil a small rectangular baking sheet. Form the mixture into a loaf shape and pour the oil on top. Cover loosely with a cap of foil and bake, 190°C/375°F/Gas Mark 5 for 35 minutes. Turn out on to a serving dish and garnish the top with lemon and cucumber slices. Serve with Juniper Sauce, but serve the sauce separately.

Juniper Sauce

1 tbsp cold-pressed safflower or
   sunflower oil
175g (6 oz) shallots or onion,
   finely chopped
1 clove garlic, crushed
10 juniper berries, crushed
225g (8 oz) fresh ripe tomatoes,
   skinned and chopped

6 large basil leaves or 1 level tsp
   dried
1 bay leaf
5 tbsps water
1 rounded tsp vegetable
   bouillon powder
freshly ground black pepper to
   taste

Heat the oil in a non-stick saucepan. Sauté the shallots or onion and garlic for 5 minutes then add the juniper berries, tomatoes, basil, bay leaf and water. To concentrate the flavour cook the sauce on a moderate to high heat stirring constantly until the sauce thickens and reduces by one third. (You can reduce the sauce by the traditional long cooking method simply by simmering on a low heat with the lid half off for approximately 30 minutes.) When reduced, taste and stir in the vegetable bouillon powder and freshly ground black pepper. Take out the bay leaf. If you want a smooth textured sauce then liquidize.

Yoghurt Cream Potatoes

450g (1 lb) potatoes, scrubbed
25g (1 oz) polyunsaturated
   margarine
1 generous tbsp Greek plain
   yoghurt

sea salt and freshly ground
   black pepper
freshly grated nutmeg or ground
   mace
little chopped parsley and mint
   to garnish

Steam the potatoes until cooked (leave whole to keep flavour in), testing with a sharp knife to see if they are cooked right through. Peel and mash with the margarine and yoghurt. Season with a little sea salt, fresh ground black pepper and a little nutmeg or mace. Cream well together. Scoop into a warm serving dish, swirl the top and sprinkle on very finely chopped parsley and mint to garnish.

Brussels Sprouts with Carrots

These two vegetables can be steamed without salt or any other seasoning as the juniper sauce is very flavoursome and will complement the fresh natural flavour of the vegetables. Cook as near to serving time as possible.

2 good size carrots, scrubbed and scraped

225g (8 oz) young Brussels sprouts, trimmed and washed
little margarine to dot the top

Cut the carrots in long slanting ovals about 5mm (¼ in) thick and place in the bottom of a steamer (or colander which fits snugly around the rim of a saucepan). Steam for 5 minutes. Place the sprouts on top (if young sprouts there is no need to slit) and steam for about 4 or 5 minutes more. Put into a warm dish and serve as soon as possible. Dot the top with a little polyunsaturated margarine.

Cinnamon Apples with Blackberry Sauce

2 large Bramley cooking apples
2 tbsps water
1 level tsp clear honey
2 tbsps apple juice concentrate
½ level tsp ground cinnamon

good pinch clove powder
175g (6 oz) blackberries, washed and drained
apple mint or lemon balm leaves to garnish (optional)

Wash and cut apples in quarters, core and slice in thin wedges (leave skins on). Heat water, honey, apple juice concentrate, cinnamon and clove powder in a non-stick frying pan. Place apple wedges in the pan, spreading them evenly over the hot liquid and poach on gentle heat for about 3 minutes only. Do not let them get mushy. Take out with a slotted spoon and arrange on a flattish serving dish. Save a few blackberries for garnish and poach the remainder in the cooking juices for 3 minutes. Press the blackberries and cooking juice through a fine sieve and extract as much purée and juice as possible. Reheat and pour over the apples.

This dessert can be eaten hot or chilled. Garnish with a sprig of apple mint or lemon balm and a few whole blackberries.

Autumn Menu for Vegans

Omit the egg from the Chick Pea Bake (page 44), stir 1 dessertspoon buckwheat flour into the lemon juice and mix with the other ingredients.

Omit the yoghurt from the Yoghurt Cream Potatoes (page 45) and use either soya milk or soya milk yoghurt (see page 15) instead.

The rest of the menu remains the same.

Autumn Menu for Meat Lovers

Instead of the Chick Pea Bake I am giving a recipe for Chicken and Broccoli Terrine which is great served with the Juniper Sauce. Again this is delicious hot or cold and the recipe for the terrine will give plenty to serve with salad for a light lunch for two the following day.

See notes on Free-range Meat (page 27).

Chicken and Broccoli Terrine

350g (12 oz) raw chicken meat,
 minced
1 small onion, minced
1 clove garlic, crushed
1 rounded tbsp wholemeal
 breadcumbs
1 large egg
2 tbsps Greek plain yoghurt

½ tsp dried rosemary
little sea salt and freshly ground
 black pepper
225g (8 oz) broccoli spears,
 lightly steamed for 3 mins.
 and finely chopped
watercress to garnish

Mix all the ingredients together except for the broccoli and press well together. Oil a 450g (1 lb) round or rectangular baking tin. Spread a third of the mixture on the bottom then spread half the chopped broccoli over this. Repeat with another layer of chicken and the remaining broccoli, finishing off with the remainder of the chicken. Cover the tin with foil. Pour water into a roasting tin almost to the top and stand the terrine in the centre. Bake, 180°c/350°F/Gas Mark 4 for 1½ hours. Let the cooked terrine stand for 5 minutes before turning out on to a serving dish. Garnish with watercress.

Serve with Juniper Sauce (see page 45).

❀ VEGETARIAN ❀

Melon Bowl Surprise
Almond, Pistachio and Bulgur Loaf
Mushroom Sauce
Sautéed Red or White Cabbage with Coriander
Roast Potatoes
Baked Apples with Fig and Aniseed Stuffing

Melon Bowl Surprise

1 Ogen or Galia melon
2 good size ripe tomatoes,
  skinned and chopped
2 tbsps cold-pressed olive or
  sunflower oil
1 tbsp lemon juice
1 clove garlic, peeled and
  crushed
¼ level tsp Dijon mustard
¼ tsp honey (optional)

¼ level tsp sea salt (or less)
few drops Tabasco sauce
freshly ground black pepper
½ tsp dried basil or rounded tsp
  fresh, chopped
½ tsp dried tarragon or
  rounded tsp fresh, chopped
(If using fresh herbs then
  reserve 2 sprigs of each to
  garnish)

Cut the melon in half widthwise and remove the seeds. Scoop out the flesh, chop and place in a bowl with the chopped tomatoes. Put the oil, lemon juice, garlic, mustard, honey, Tabasco, salt, pepper, basil and tarragon in a screw-top jar and shake well. Pour this over the melon and tomatoes and let marinate in the 'fridge for 20 minutes. Spoon into the melon case halves and keep chilled until ready to serve.

If using fresh herbs then garnish with a sprig of basil and tarragon in each half.

Almond, Pistachio and Bulgur Loaf

50g (2 oz) bulgur wheat
100ml (4 fl oz) boiling water
1 rounded tsp vegetable
  bouillon powder
110g (4 oz) almonds
50g (2 oz) pistachio nuts (weight
  when shelled)

1 small onion, finely chopped
1 level tsp lemon thyme
1 tbsp finely chopped parsley
1 standard egg
1 tbsp cold-pressed sunflower
  or olive oil
little more oil for roasting

Put bulgur in a small mixing bowl. Mix the boiling water with the bouillon powder and pour over the bulgur, cover and leave to swell for 20 minutes. Meanwhile, grind the almonds and pistachios until they are like medium fine breadcrumbs (not powdery). Stir in the chopped onion, parsley, lemon thyme, egg and the oil. When bulgur is ready add it to the almond mixture. Mould well together with your hands and form into a loaf shape. Lightly oil a roasting tin and place the loaf in the centre. Sprinkle on a little oil and cap loosely with baking foil. This is cooked with the recipe for roast potatoes overleaf.

Mushroom Sauce

110g (4 oz) small button mushrooms

1 tbsp oil from the roasting loaf and potato tin

¼ tsp freshly ground coriander seeds

275ml (10 fl oz) stock (use the drained potato liquid from recipe overleaf)

1 level tbsp unbleached white flour

1 rounded tbsp Greek plain yoghurt

50ml (2 fl oz) white wine (optional but delicious)

freshly ground black pepper to taste

little sea salt if necessary (taste before adding)

Rinse and wipe the mushrooms, slice thinly. Heat the oil in a medium size non-stick saucepan. Fry the mushrooms with the coriander on a gentle heat for 4 minutes. Put 2 tablespoons of the cooled stock in a small mixing bowl blending in the flour and yoghurt to make a smooth runny paste. Add the rest of the stock to the mushrooms and bring to the boil. Blend a little of this hot liquid with the flour mixture and gradually pour this into the mushroom broth stirring constantly as you do so. Cook on a gentle heat for 3 minutes. Finally, stir in the wine and black pepper, taste and add sea salt if necessary.

Sautéed Red or White Cabbage with Coriander

350g (12 oz) red or white
  cabbage, shredded
little sea salt

3 tsps cold-pressed sunflower oil
½ tsp coriander seeds, crushed

Bring 275ml (½ pint) water to boil, add ¼ teaspoon sea salt and drop in the shredded cabbage. Cook for just 1 minute. Drain in a colander and sprinkle cold water all over.

When ready to serve heat the oil in a pan, fry the crushed coriander for half a minute, add the drained cabbage and stir-fry on moderate heat for just 2 minutes. The cabbage will be cooked but still crisp.

Roast Potatoes

By par-boiling the potatoes with the other ingredients listed here you will have a simple tasty stock to make the mushroom sauce.

5 medium size potatoes,
  scrubbed and cut in quarters
1 medium size carrot, scrubbed
  and cut in small pieces

1 stick celery, chopped
1 small onion, cut in thin rings
2 sprigs parsley
¼ level tsp sea salt

Put all the ingredients into a medium size saucepan and just cover with boiling water. Bring to boil, turn down to simmer, cover and cook for 8 minutes. Take out potatoes with a slotted spoon, peel skins off and return skins to the broth. Cover broth and leave to one side.

Arrange potatoes around the nut loaf, sprinkle a little oil on each potato and bake, 190°c/375°F/Gas Mark 5 for 40 minutes. Take foil cap off the nut loaf 10 minutes before end of cooking time.

Baked Apples with Fig and Aniseed Stuffing

2 large cooking apples, cored
4 dried figs, trimmed and
* washed*
1 tbsp clear honey

juice and grated rind of 1 small
* orange*
½ level tsp ground aniseed
25g (1 oz) chopped nuts

Chop the figs and place in a small bowl. Mix the honey with a little hot water to soak the chopped figs in and leave for a few hours. Drain and reserve the liquid. In a blender, process the soaked figs with the orange rind, juice and aniseed for just a few seconds (do not make too smooth). Stir in the chopped nuts.

Place the apples in a small greased ovenproof dish and stuff with the fig mixture. Pour the soaking liquid over the apples and bake, 180°C/350°F/Gas Mark 4, for 45 minutes to 1 hour. Baste the apples several times during the cooking period.

Winter Menu for Vegans

In the recipe for Almond, Pistachio and Bulgur Loaf (page 50), omit the egg and mix 1 level tablespoon of buckwheat flour with a little cold water until smooth and blend into the other ingredients.

Omit the yoghurt from the Mushroom Sauce (page 52) and use 2 tablespoons of soya milk or soya milk yoghurt (see page 15) instead.

The rest of the menu remains the same.

Winter Menu for Meat Lovers

Follow the menu for vegetarian but substitute the Almond, Pistachio and Bulgur Loaf with Chicken, Pistachio and Bulgur Loaf. Here is a very tasty recipe for this.

You will note that the potatoes are par-boiled with the chicken and other ingredients which will give you a delicious stock for the Mushroom Sauce.

Chicken, Pistachio and Bulgur Loaf

TO COOK THE CHICKEN:

approx. 400g (14 oz) chicken
   joint on the bone (this will
   give you approx. 225g (8 oz)
   chicken)
1 small onion cut in thin rings
1 medium size carrot, scrubbed
   and cut in small pieces

1 stick celery, chopped
large sprig parsley
5 medium size potatoes,
   scrubbed and cut in quarters
425ml (¾ pint) boiling water
¼ tsp sea salt
freshly ground black pepper

Place all the ingredients in a medium size saucepan and cover with boiling water. Bring to boil and simmer with the lid on for 8 minutes only. Take out the potatoes with a slotted spoon, peel off the skins and pop the skins back into the saucepan. Continue to cook the chicken for a further 10 minutes. Take out the chicken, cover the broth and leave to one side for making the Mushroom Sauce as instructed on page 52. Bone the chicken and mince the flesh.

FOR THE LOAF:

50g (2 oz) bulgur wheat
100ml (4 fl oz) boiling water
1 rounded tsp vegetable
   bouillon powder
50g (2 oz) pistachio nuts,
   ground

1 small onion, finely chopped
1 tbsp fresh parsley, chopped
1 level tsp lemon thyme
1 standard egg
1 tbsp cold-pressed oil
little oil for roasting

Prepare as for vegetarian Almond, Pistachio and Bulgur Loaf and bake in the same way.

Formal Dinner Parties

Friendship and eating good food are two of the greatest joys of life: giving a dinner party means you can indulge in a double pleasure. 'Formal' may conjure up an idea of stiffness and over-elaborate food, but I simply mean a sit-down meal with several courses for 6 to 8 people, with my guests being as informal as they wish.

As you carefully prepare the food and adorn the table with candles and flowers, turn on your favourite music and enjoy the sheer delight of entertaining with healthy delicious food. In this mood you can't fail!

_____ Spring Menu _____

❀ VEGETARIAN ❀

Baby Courgettes in Red Chicory Beds with
Pimento and Garlic Dressing
Spring Vegetable Pie
New Potatoes with Mint
Tomato, Orange, Spring Onion & Watercress Salad
Maple, Banana, Rum & Pecan Nut
Ice Cream
Mould with Fresh Pineapple

_____ ❀ _____

Baby Courgettes in Red Chicory Beds with Pimento and Garlic Dressing

This dish is best made a few hours before serving so that the dressing penetrates the steamed courgettes.

1.2kg (2½ lbs) baby courgettes, leave whole

1 head of red chicory (radicchio)

PIMENTO AND GARLIC DRESSING:

2 medium size red peppers, deseeded

5 tbsps cold-pressed sesame or olive oil

4 tbsps lemon juice

2 large cloves garlic, crushed

1 rounded tsp dried oregano

little sea salt and freshly ground black pepper

Steam the whole red peppers and courgettes until tender but not mushy. Rinse in cold water and pat dry. Place the courgettes in a shallow bowl. In a food processor or liquidizer blend red peppers with the other ingredients, mix well together and pour over the courgettes. Allow to marinate for 2 hours, turning them occasionally.

Separate the leaves of the red chicory, wash and pat dry. Place one leaf in each of the 8 individual shallow serving bowls. Spoon on the marinated courgettes and pour the dressing on top.

Spring Vegetable Pie

You can vary the vegetables in this recipe using less expensive ones when not entertaining. I think the choice here blends well together to give a delicious flavour. I have used dried flageolet beans (see page 20) to balance the protein of the dish. These young light green beans have a delicate flavour which complements the other vegetables rather than overpowers them.

FILLING:

170g (6 oz) flageolet beans
225g (8 oz) asparagus (woody ends removed before weighing)
½ fennel bulb, outer skin scraped then finely chopped
6 baby onions, scrubbed and chopped
6 young carrots, scrubbed and chopped
1 celery heart, chopped
900ml (1½ pints) boiling water
1 bay leaf
1 tbsp vegetable bouillon powder
2 tbsps lemon juice
1 tsp oregano
1 tsp dried tarragon
110g (4 oz) small button mushrooms, leave whole
1 small red pepper, deseeded and chopped
225g (8 oz) young spinach leaves

1 level tsp ground mace or nutmeg
2 tbsps cold-pressed sunflower oil
75g (3 oz) unbleached white flour
200ml (7 fl oz) dry white wine
1 rounded tbsp soylk (pre-cooked soya flour)
225g (8 oz) quark
freshly ground black pepper
2 tbsps very finely chopped parsley

CHEESE PASTRY TOPPING:

350g (12 oz) wholemeal flour, plain
170g (6 oz) polyunsaturated margarine
4½ tbsps cold water
50g (2 oz) Gruyère cheese, finely grated
good pinch sea salt (optional)
little beaten egg for glazing

For the filling:

Soak the beans overnight changing the water 3 times. Rinse and cook in fresh water. Boil vigorously for 10 minutes then simmer for about 50 minutes or until the beans are cooked. (If adding salt, do this 10 minutes before the end of cooking time.) Drain and leave to cool. Cut off the tips of the asparagus and leave to one side. Chop the stems and place these, the fennel, onion, carrots, and celery in a large heavy-based saucepan. Pour on the boiling water and add the bay leaf, vegetable bouillon powder, lemon juice and herbs. Cook for just 5 minutes. Add the asparagus tips, whole mushrooms, red pepper and spinach and cook for a further 2 minutes. All the vegetables should still be firm. Drain and reserve the liquid. Mix the vegetables with the flageolet beans and leave to cool. Your liquid should measure 700ml (1¼ pints), add mace.

Heat the oil in a non-stick saucepan and using a wooden

spoon stir in the unbleached white flour and cook, stirring constantly, for 1 minute. Still stirring, gradually add the hot stock and cook until the sauce thickens. Stir in the white wine and when incorporated take off the heat. Blend the soya flour with the quark until smooth. Add a little of the hot sauce to this then add the quark mixture to the rest of the sauce. Reheat but do not boil. (The sauce will continue to cook in the oven.) Take off the heat and season with freshly ground black pepper and add the parsley. Stir the sauce into the cooked vegetables and place the lot in an oiled pie dish about 25cm (10 in) square or 30cm (12 in) round. Allow to cool. Preheat the oven to 190°c/ 375°F/Gas Mark 5.

To make the pastry:
Sieve the flour. In a mixing bowl cream the margarine with the water and 4 tablespoons of the flour until smooth and well blended. Stir in the cheese, and the salt if using. Gradually add the rest of the flour using your hands to form a smooth dough. Knead for 2 minutes. Put into a plastic bag and chill for 30 minutes. Roll out on a lightly floured surface. Lifting the pastry up on to the rolling pin cover your filling, crimp the edges and use the trimmings to decorate the top with leaves and asparagus tip shapes. Stick these on with a little beaten egg and then brush the whole of the top. Bake in the preheated oven for 30 minutes until the pastry is a golden brown on top.

Tomato, Orange, Spring Onion & Watercress Salad

450g (1 lb) tomatoes, thinly sliced
4 oranges, peeled and thinly sliced
1 bunch spring onions, trimmed and chopped finely

2 bunches watercress, washed well
Dressing as for Fresh Green Salad (page 100)

In a shallow serving dish spread out the watercress sprigs. Arrange the tomato and orange slices overlapping in 2 circles on top of the cress. Sprinkle over the chopped spring onions and pour over the dressing.

Maple, Banana, Rum & Pecan Nut Ice Cream Mould with Fresh Pineapple

You can make this well in advance. Use pure maple syrup as some are made with sugar and maple flavouring.

170ml (6 fl oz) pure maple syrup
6 large bananas
2 tbsps lemon juice
350g (12 oz) Greek plain yoghurt
2 tbsps rum
50g (2 oz) pecan nuts, roughly chopped

2 egg whites
1 medium size pineapple
FOR POURING OVER FRUIT AND MOULD:
3 tbsps pure maple syrup
1 tbsp rum
25g (1 oz) pecan nut halves to decorate

Warm the maple syrup on gentle heat. Purée the bananas in a blender with the lemon juice. Pour in the warm syrup and blend well together. Add the yoghurt and rum and blend again. Spoon into a bowl and stir in the pecan nuts. Whisk the egg whites until they form stiff peaks, then fold this into the banana mixture. Spoon into a shallow freezer tray, cover with foil and freeze for 3 hours. Take out and blend again in a mixer (make sure the bowl is cold).

Freeze again in the shallow tray and blend after 2 hours. Spoon the beaten mixture into a 1.1 litre (2 pint) savarin mould, cover with foil and freeze. Slice the ends off the pineapple, remove the skin and take out the tough eyes with a sharp pointed knife. Cut into small chunks.

To serve, take the banana ice cream mixture out of the freezer, loosen the edges from the mould with a warm, sharp knife, dip the mould into warm water for a few seconds and turn out on to a flat serving dish. Pile the pineapple chunks into the centre. Mix the maple syrup and rum together and pour over the top of the fruit and mould. Decorate with the pecan nut halves.

Spring Menu for Vegans

In the recipe for Spring Vegetable Pie (page 56) omit the quark and use just under 275ml (½ pint) soya milk instead. Omit the cheese from the pastry and add 2 tablespoons of sesame seeds.

In the recipe for Maple, Banana, Rum and Pecan Nut Ice Cream Mould (page 59) use either 350g (12 oz) soya yoghurt (see page 15) or silken tofu (page 17) and omit the egg whites. As there will be less fat content you will need to whisk the semi-frozen mixture 3 times before placing in the savarin mould for the final freezing.

The rest of the menu remains the same.

Spring Menu for Meat Lovers

Instead of Spring Vegetable Pie (page 56) do the following recipe.

Spring Vegetable and Chicken Pie

Omit the flageolet beans from the vegetarian recipe and use instead 900g (2 lbs) of chicken joints. Skin the joints and boil them in the 900ml (1½ pints) water and vegetable bouillon powder until tender. Bone the joints and chop the meat into 3.5cm (1½ in) slivers. Leave to one side and cook the vegetables in the chicken stock to which you will have to add more water to bring it to the 900ml (1½ pints) level. Also, use sour cream instead of the quark following exactly the same instructions as in the Spring Vegetable Pie recipe (page 56). Stir the cooked, chopped chicken into the sauce and vegetable mixture, top with the pastry and bake as previously instructed.

The rest of the menu remains the same.

❀ VEGETARIAN ❀

Nori-wrapped Vegetable Moulds with
Carrot and Yoghurt Sauce
Sprouted Lentil Fettuccini Bake
Beetroot, Fennel and Mint Salad
Tipsy Apricot Cheese Pie

Nori-wrapped Vegetable Moulds with Carrot and Yoghurt Sauce

❀

Nori is a sea vegetable and comes in paper thin sheets (see page 22).
You can use frozen peas or broad beans but the taste of freshly podded is much more flavoursome.
Make these 8 hours before serving as they have to be well chilled. You will need 8 ramekin dishes.

350g (12 oz) fresh peas or young broad beans (weight when podded)
175g (6 oz) frozen sweetcorn kernels
2 large avocados, peeled, stoned and finely chopped
2 small red sweet peppers, deseeded and finely chopped
3 tbsps chives, chopped (you can use spring onions)
2 tbsps cold-pressed olive oil
2 tbsps lemon juice
freshly ground black pepper and sea salt to taste
few sprigs of parsley to garnish
8 sheets of nori

Cook the peas or broad beans in lightly salted water until tender. If young then this should only take 5 minutes. Drain. Cook the sweetcorn in the pea or bean cooking water for 3 minutes only then drain. Process the peas or beans in a liquidizer or food processor until a medium smooth texture is obtained (do not use any water to purée the mixture as it must be slightly rough and dryish). Scoop out and place in a mixing bowl. Stir in the cooked sweetcorn, chopped avocados, chopped red pepper, chives, oil and lemon juice, seasoning well with a little sea salt and freshly ground black pepper to your taste.

Dampen each nori sheet with a little lukewarm water. Line each ramekin dish with 1 sheet, it will drape over the edge and cover the filling easily. Spoon in equal amounts of the vegetable mixture and fold over the nori to seal the filling in completely. Press the nori down gently with wet fingers. Chill for 8 hours.

To serve, turn out the Nori Moulds on to individual serving plates and spoon around a little of the Carrot and Yoghurt Sauce (page 63).

Carrot and Yoghurt Sauce

This sauce is very simple to prepare and a light and delicious complement to the Nori Moulds (page 62).

225g (8 oz) carrots, washed and
  scraped
250ml (8 fl oz) water
½ vegetable stock cube
1 small bay leaf
1 tsp caraway seeds, tied in a
  piece of muslin

2 tbsps Greek plain yoghurt
juice of half a lemon
2 tbsps white wine
sea salt and freshly ground
  black pepper to taste

Chop the carrots into medium size chunks. Boil the water with the half stock cube, bay leaf and tied-up caraway seeds and allow to simmer with the lid off for 5 minutes. Drop in the carrots and cook until they are tender. Remove the bay leaf and caraway seeds. Liquidize the carrots with a little of the cooking liquid and add the yoghurt, lemon juice and wine. Taste and season with sea salt and, if necessary, freshly ground black pepper.

This can be served hot or cold but it is best cold when served with the Nori Moulds.

Sprouted Lentil Fettuccini Bake

I first tasted fettuccini swirled into a mould and filled with a rich cream and mushroom sauce 20 years ago in Italy.
Needless to say there were no sprouted lentils in the recipe but I don't think the addition of these detracts from the lovely flavour of this delicious and easy-to-prepare dish.
You will need 2 1.4 litre (2½ pint) capacity timbale moulds or ovenproof pudding basins. The lentils need to be started for sprouting 4 days before needed (see page 12).

350g (12 oz) sprouted weight whole green lentils
2 tbsps cold-pressed sunflower or olive oil
2 large cloves garlic, crushed
1 large onion, peeled and finely chopped
1 rounded tsp coriander seeds, finely ground
350g (12 oz) small button mushrooms
2 tbsps fresh chopped marjoram or basil or 1 rounded tsp dried
2 tbsps tomato purée
50g (2 oz) unbleached white flour
225g (8 oz) carton of Greek plain yoghurt
1 rounded tbsp vegetable bouillon powder
6 tbsps dry sherry
275ml (½ pint) cold water
freshly ground black pepper to taste
450g (1 lb) fettuccini
freshly grated Parmesan or Pecorino cheese to serve

Sprout the whole green lentils as directed on page 12 for 4 days. Rinse and drain, then pat dry.

Heat the oil in a large frying pan and sweat the garlic and onion on gentle heat for 6 minutes. Add the lentil sprouts and coriander and stir-fry for 3 minutes. Add the mushrooms and marjoram or basil and stir-fry for a further 3 minutes. In a blender process the tomato purée, flour, yoghurt, vegetable bouillon powder, sherry and water until smooth. Pour into the vegetable mixture and cook, stirring constantly until the sauce thickens. Add freshly ground black pepper to your taste and remove from heat.

Bring a large saucepan of slightly salted water to boil. Cook the fettuccini until almost soft (see directions on the packet and cook for a few minutes less than stated). Drain and trickle on a little oil to stop the noodles sticking together. Allow to cool enough to handle.

Oil the 2 dishes and line the bottom and sides generously with the fettuccini, swirling it around as you do this. Stir the remaining fettuccini into the vegetable sauce and spoon this into the fettuccini-lined dishes. Cover with a saucer, then foil, and bake at 190°c/375°f/Gas Mark 5 for about 35 to 40 minutes. Allow to stand for 5 minutes before turning out on to warm serving dishes.

Beetroot, Fennel and Mint Salad

700g (1½ lbs) raw beetroot,
  peeled and grated
1 good size fennel bulb, scraped
  and grated
6 medium size tomatoes, cut
  into thin wedges
6 spring onions, trimmed and
  finely chopped

1 tbsp fresh mint, chopped
4 tbsps cold-pressed sunflower
  or olive oil
2 tbsps lemon juice
¼ tsp sea salt
¼ tsp freshly ground black
  pepper
1 bunch watercress, chopped

Mix all the ingredients together except the watercress and chill
for 1 hour before serving.
  When ready to serve stir in the chopped watercress.

Tipsy Apricot Cheese Pie

For best results, this delicious low fat cheese pie has to be
made 24 hours before serving. In the morning the day
before, marinate the apricots as described below and in the
evening, make the pie.

12 ripe fresh apricots (not too
  soft)
2 tbsps brandy
2 tsps pulpy juice from freshly
  grated ginger root
1 tbsp fruit sugar
SWEET BISCUIT PASTRY BASE:
50g (2 oz) ground almonds
½ tsp ground cinnamon
170g (6 oz) 100% wholemeal
  flour, plain
pinch sea salt
110g (4 oz) polyunsaturated
  margarine

40g (1½ oz) fruit sugar
2 tbsps cold water
1 large egg yolk
FILLING:
350g (12 oz) goat's curd or
  ricotta cheese
110g (4 oz) Greek plain yoghurt
3 level tbsps clear honey
3 drops of natural vanilla
  essence
grated rind of 1 lemon
25g (1 oz) flaked and toasted
  almonds

To marinate the fruit:
Dip the apricots in boiling water and leave for 1 minute. Peel off skins, cut in half and stone, then slice in wedges. Grate the fresh ginger root and press the pulp through a sieve until you have 2 teaspoons of thinnish juicy pulp. Stir this into the brandy with the fruit sugar. Arrange the apricot slices in a fluted dish and pour over the brandy mixture, cover and leave for 8 hours.

To make the biscuit base:
Sieve the ground almonds, cinnamon, flour and salt into a mixing bowl. Cream the margarine and sugar in another mixing bowl for 2 minutes. Whisk the water with the egg yolk until frothy and add to the creamed mixture with 2 teaspoons of the flour mixture. Blend well together gradually adding the rest of the dry ingredients. Using your hands to form into a dough knead for 1 minute, place in a polythene bag and chill for 1 hour.

Preheat oven to 190°c/375°F/Gas Mark 5. Roll out the dough on a lightly floured surface, lift on to the rolling pin and use to line a 25cm (10 in) well greased, loose-bottomed, shallow fluted baking tin. Prick the base and bake for 20 minutes on the middle shelf. Cover loosely with greaseproof paper if it is browning too quickly. Leave to get completely cold.

For the filling:
In a blender put the cheese, yoghurt, honey, vanilla essence and lemon rind and process for a few seconds until smooth. Spoon into a bowl, stir in three-quarters of the marinated apricot slices (reserving the juice). Loosen the pastry case carefully from the tin and ease on to a flat serving dish. Spoon the cheese mixture into the cold pastry case decorating the top with the remaining apricot slices and the toasted almonds. Put the marinating juice into a small jug and let your guests serve themselves to a little of this over their individual portion if they wish.

Summer Menu for Vegans

Omit the yoghurt from the Carrot and Yoghurt Sauce (page 63) and purée with a little more carrot cooking liquid and an extra tablespoon of lemon juice or use soya milk yoghurt (page 15).

In the recipe for Sprouted Lentil Fettuccini Bake (page 63) use 225g (8 oz) firm tofu instead of the Greek plain yoghurt.

Instead of the Tipsy Apricot Cheese Pie (page 65) do the following recipe.

Tipsy Apricot Tofu Cream Pie

Prepare and marinate the apricots as in the Tipsy Apricot Cheese Pie recipe (page 65). Omit the egg yolk from the biscuit pastry base and use 3 tablespoons of water instead of 2. Prepare and bake blind as directed. Allow to cool.

TOFU CREAM FILLING:
450g (1 lb) firm tofu
4 tbsps clear honey
4 tbsps of the apricot marinating liquid
few drops of natural vanilla essence
grated rind of 1 lemon
2 tbsps lemon juice
25g (1 oz) flaked almonds

Preheat the oven to 180°C/350°F/Gas Mark 4. Blend all the ingredients in a liquidizer or food processor. Stir in three-quarters of the marinated apricot slices. Spoon the tofu and fruit mixture into the cooked pastry case and sprinkle on the flaked almonds. Bake in the centre of the oven for 1 hour. Cool and then chill. Loosen from the tin and ease on to a serving plate, decorate with the remaining apricot slices just before serving.

The rest of the menu remains the same.

Summer Menu for Meat Lovers

Instead of the recipe for Nori-wrapped Vegetable Moulds (page 62) you can do an equally tasty starter using sea food with vegetables.

Nori-wrapped Sea Food and Vegetable Moulds

8 sheets of nori

175g (6 oz) fresh peas or young broad beans (weight when podded)

2 large avocados, peeled, stoned and chopped in small pieces

2 small red sweet peppers, deseeded and finely chopped

3 tbsps chives, finely chopped (you can use spring onions)

2 tbsps cold-pressed olive oil

2 tbsps lemon juice

110g (4 oz) prawns, finely chopped

110g (4 oz) crab meat

110g (4 oz) scallops, lightly steamed for 5 mins. and chopped

2 tsps shoyu (naturally fermented soya sauce)

Cook the peas or broad beans in lightly salted water until tender. If young they should take only 5 minutes. Drain and purée in a blender or food processor with the avocados for a few seconds only (do not make too smooth). Mix with all the other ingredients and follow the instructions for lining, filling and chilling the ramekin dishes as in the vegetarian menu.

Instead of Sprouted Lentil Fettuccini Bake (page 63) do the following recipe for:

Mushroom and Minced Meat Fettuccini Bake

Follow the vegetarian recipe (page 63) but use 350g (12 oz) cooked, chopped meat instead of the sprouted lentils. A good choice would be 175g (6 oz) each of either lamb and ham, rabbit and ham or chicken and ham.

The rest of the menu remains the same.

❀ VEGETARIAN ❀

*Lettuce, Avocado and Tangerine Starter with
Tangy Vinaigrette
Pumpkin in Molee Curry Sauce
Tempura Vegetables
Saffron Rice with Almonds and Sweetcorn
Cucumber, Mint and Yoghurt Cooler
Autumn Fruit and Port Pudding*

Lettuce, Avocado and Tangerine Starter with Tangy Vinaigrette

1 good size Iceberg lettuce or 2 small

2 medium size avocados

3 tangerines

4 spring onions, very finely chopped (use green ends)

TANGY VINAIGRETTE:

1 tbsp tangerine juice

5 tbsps cold-pressed sunflower or olive oil

1 tbsp lime juice (lemon will do)

½ tsp Dijon mustard

½ tsp clear honey

1 tsp capers, well rinsed and patted dry

1 small clove garlic, crushed

Wash lettuce and break off 8 outer leaves arranging these leaves in a large shallow serving dish. Shred the remaining lettuce hearts. Peel and stone the avocados and cut into thin slices (sprinkling on a little lemon juice to stop them browning). Peel the tangerines, remove the pith and divide into segments. Spoon the shredded lettuce into the outer lettuce leaves and arrange the tangerine and avocado slices decoratively on top. Sprinkle on the chopped spring onions.

Blend all the vinaigrette ingredients in a liquidizer or food processor and pour over the individually filled lettuce leaves.

Pumpkin in Molee Curry Sauce (Light Coconut Milk Curry)

This South Indian sauce made with coconut milk can be served with sautéed mixed vegetables, lightly poached fish or thin slivers of meat. Here I have used pumpkin which absorbs the flavour of the sauce beautifully and is a delicious way to serve this much neglected vegetable. (The sauce can be made hotter by adding more cayenne pepper if you like hot curries.)

To make coconut milk (see page 17), you can use either a mixture of cow's, goat's or soya milk and water, as they all end up with a similar flavour.

900g (2 lbs) pumpkin, peeled, deseeded and cut into 2.5cm (1 in) cubes

MOLEE CURRY SAUCE:

40g (1½ oz) piece of tamarind

3 tbsps cold-pressed sunflower oil

2 large onions, peeled and very finely chopped

4 large cloves garlic, crushed

1 tsp fennel seed, crushed

seeds from 4 cardamom pods, crushed

1 tsp black mustard seeds

2 rounded tbsps gram flour (chick pea flour)

1 level tsp turmeric

1 rounded tsp ground coriander

1 level tsp ground cumin

1 tsp cayenne pepper

¼ level tsp clove powder

2 tsps fresh ginger, grated

2 tsps methi (fenugreek leaf)

8 canned tomatoes, puréed and sieved

700ml (1¼ pints) thick coconut milk (page 17)

little sea salt to taste

Steam the pumpkin cubes until tender but still firm (this takes about 10 minutes).

For the Molee Curry Sauce:
Sauté the tamarind in 4 tablespoons of hot water for 20 minutes. Press through a sieve and extract as much pulp as possible. Heat oil in a large saucepan and sauté the onion and garlic for 10 minutes until soft (do not brown). Make a space in the centre and add the fennel seeds, crushed cardamom seeds and black mustard seeds and fry on a low heat for 2 minutes. Mix the gram flour, turmeric, coriander powder, cumin powder, clove powder, cayenne and ginger to a smooth paste with the tamarind pulp and a little cold water. Stir this with the fenugreek leaf into the onion mixture and cook on a very gentle heat for 3 minutes. Gradually add to this the puréed and sieved tomatoes and the coconut milk stirring constantly to avoid lumps. Cook for 10 minutes on a gentle heat and then remove to one side. Marinate the steamed pumpkin in this sauce for at least 1 hour or longer, reheating on a low temperature just before serving.
Note: You can make the sauce well in advance and freeze. To serve, defrost the sauce, heat slowly and marinate the pumpkin or other vegetables in the hot sauce as above.

Tempura Vegetables

This dish is great for using up odd bits of leftover but still fresh vegetables.
450g (1 lb) of sliced mixed vegetables will give you a huge plate of deep-fried crispy battered vegetables.

450g (1 lb) mixed vegetables such as small cauliflower florets, thick onion rings, sliced carrots, courgettes and aubergines

BATTER:

175g (6 oz) gram flour (chick pea flour)

50g (2 oz) brown rice flour
1 tsp baking powder
275ml (½ pint) water
1 tsp garam masala
little sea salt
soya oil for deep frying
little shoyu (naturally fermented soya sauce) to serve

Sift flour and baking powder into a bowl and gradually add the water to make a thickish batter. Whisk well and allow to stand for half an hour. Stir in the spices and whisk well again before using. (You can blend the ingredients in a liquidizer or food processor, it takes just 30 seconds.) Heat oil to hot (do not use a chip basket). Dip the vegetables into the batter, coating them well, and deep fry until golden brown and crisp. Drain on absorbent kitchen paper and serve immediately.

Let the guests sprinkle on a little shoyu to their own taste.
(**Note:** You can prepare these in advance by deep frying until almost done, drain and put aside (do not put them into the refrigerator). Deep fry until golden when ready to serve.)

Saffron Rice with Almonds and Sweetcorn

450g (1 lb) Surinam long grain
  brown rice
2 tbsps cold-pressed sunflower
  oil
1 large onion, peeled and finely
  chopped
hot water (double the volume of
  rice)

good pinch of saffron
1 bay leaf
1 level tsp sea salt
110g (4 oz) blanched slivered
  almonds, lightly toasted
225g (8 oz) sweetcorn, cooked
  for 3 mins. only

Wash rice well by putting in a sieve and letting cold water run through the grains for half a minute, then drain well. Heat oil in a large heavy-based saucepan, add the onion and sauté for 7 minutes on a low heat with the lid on. Take off the lid, increase the heat and brown the onion (do not burn). Add the rice and continue to cook stirring constantly for a further 3 minutes. Pour in the water, add saffron, salt and bay leaf and bring to the boil, turn down to simmer, cover with a tight lid and cook for 25 minutes when the water will all have been absorbed. Finally, stir in the almonds and sweetcorn and spoon into a warm serving dish.

Cucumber, Mint and Yoghurt Cooler

1 large carton natural yoghurt
2 level tbsps fresh mint,
  chopped
1 tbsp fresh lemon juice
½ tsp clear honey
½ tsp Dijon mustard

little sea salt and freshly ground
  black pepper to taste
1 large cucumber cut in thin
  rings
sprig of mint to garnish

In a bowl blend yoghurt, mint, lemon juice, honey and mustard well together. Add sea salt and freshly ground black pepper to your taste. Arrange the cucumber in a shallow serving dish, pour over the dressing and garnish with a sprig of mint.

Autumn Fruit and Port Pudding

This pudding makes good use of the cheap fruits available in the autumn. It is in fact an autumn version of Summer Pudding.
The ingredients will fill a 1.4 litre (2½ pint) pudding basin.

10 large slices of wholemeal
   bread, crusts removed
350g (12 oz) cooking apples,
   cored, peeled and thinly
   sliced
225g (8 oz) plums halved and
   stoned
225g (8 oz) ripe juicy pears,
   peeled, cored and thinly
   sliced

175g (6 oz) blackberries
50g (2 oz) chopped pecan nuts
2 tbsps port
2 tbsps Pear and Apple Spread
¼ level tsp clove powder
½ tsp ground cinnamon
blackberries and blackberry
   leaves to garnish

Line the well oiled pudding basin with wholemeal bread slices up to about 2cm (1 in) from the top of the bowl. Mix the prepared fruit with the nuts, port, Pear and Apple Spread and spices. Carefully spoon into the bread-lined pudding basin, top with wholemeal bread. Cover the bowl tightly with foil and steam for 1¼ hours. Allow to cool and then chill in the 'fridge until completely cold. Turn out on to a serving dish and decorate with the blackberries and blackberry leaves.

Serve with Greek yoghurt or sour cream.

Autumn Menu for Vegans

In the recipe for Pumpkin in Molee Curry Sauce (page 70) the coconut milk can be made with soya milk (see page 16) for recipe.

Instead of the Cucumber, Mint and Yoghurt Cooler do the following recipe.

Cucumber, Mint and Tofu Cooler

275g (10 oz) silken tofu
2 level tbsps fresh mint,
  chopped
2 tbsps fresh lemon juice
½ tsp clear honey
½ tsp Dijon mustard

pinch sea salt
freshly ground black pepper
  (optional)
1 large cucumber, cut in thin
  rings
sprig of mint to garnish

In a mixer blend well together tofu, mint, lemon juice, honey and mustard, then add sea salt and black pepper to your taste.

Arrange the cucumber in a flattish serving dish, pour over the dressing and put a sprig of mint in the centre to garnish.

The rest of the menu remains the same.

Autumn Menu for Meat Lovers

Instead of the recipe for Pumpkin in Molee Curry Sauce (page 70) do the following recipe.

White Fish in Molee Curry Sauce

900g/1.2kg (2/2½ lbs)
  haddock, cod or halibut
  (weight when filleted)

Molee Curry Sauce (see page
  71)

Make the sauce as directed on page 71. Skin the fish and cut into approximately 5cm (2 in) long and 4cm (1½ in) wide pieces. Marinate in the cooked sauce for 1 hour then cook on a low heat for 10 minutes until the fish is tender and cooked right through.

The rest of the menu remains the same.

Winter Menu

❀ **VEGETARIAN** ❀

Chick Pea, Leek and Cabbage Soup
Corn, Cheese and Garlic Sticks
Tofu Tempura
Sweet and Sour Sauce
Baked Rice and Mushrooms
Alfalfa, Orange, Onion and Tomato Salad
Brandied Winter Fruit and Nut Salad

❀

Chick Pea, Leek and Cabbage Soup

This is a delicious mixture and just great to warm your guests on a cold winter evening.

110g (4 oz) chick peas (dry weight)
570ml (1 pint) water
½ tsp sea salt
350g (12 oz) leeks, trimmed and chopped (weight when trimmed)
1.7 litres (3 pints) water
1 rounded tsp garam masala
1 bay leaf

2 rounded tbsps vegetable bouillon powder
4 tbsps lemon juice
450g (1 lb) cabbage, very finely shredded
2 tbsps fresh parsley, chopped
freshly ground black pepper
1 tbsp cold-pressed sesame oil
1 tbsp fresh mint, chopped or 1 tsp dried
1 level tsp fennel seeds

Soak the chick peas overnight changing the water 3 times. Rinse and bring to boil with 575ml (1 pint) cold water. Boil vigorously for 10 minutes then turn down to simmer. Cover and cook for 50 minutes or until soft, adding a little sea salt 10 minutes before the end of the cooking time. Liquidize with the cooking liquid until smooth.

Put leeks, the 1.7 litres (3 pints) of water, vegetable bouillon powder and garam masala together with the bay leaf into a large saucepan. Bring to boil, turn down to simmer, cover and cook for 15 minutes only. Take out bay leaf. Liquidize until smooth and put back into the saucepan. Stir in the chick pea purée and blend well together. Bring to boil and add the lemon juice, shredded cabbage and parsley. Cook on moderate heat for 1½ minutes only.

When ready to serve, heat the soup, then heat the oil in a frying pan and fry the chopped mint and fennel seeds for 1½ minutes on moderate heat. Pour the hot soup into a serving dish and spoon on the fried mint and fennel seeds.

Corn, Cheese and Garlic Sticks

———————— Makes 14 ————————

You will need either a corn stick tray or an éclair tray but if
these are not available then muffin trays will do.

3 tbsps cold-pressed corn or
 sunflower oil
75g (3 oz) onion, finely
 chopped
1 large egg
200ml (7 fl oz) milk or milk and
 yoghurt mixed
2 large cloves garlic, crushed
1 generous tbsp honey or malt
 extract

110g (4 oz) 81% wheatmeal
 flour
150g (3 oz) yellow cornmeal
1 level tbsp baking powder
2 tsps vegetable bouillon
 powder
175g (6 oz) fresh or frozen corn
 kernels
50g (2 oz) Cheddar cheese,
 grated

Preheat oven to 220°c/425°F/Gas Mark 7.

Heat the oil in a small frying pan and sauté the onion on a
gentle heat until soft and transparent, cool. Beat the egg, milk,
honey and crushed garlic together. Blend flour, cornmeal,
baking powder and vegetable bouillon powder in a mixing
bowl. (If using frozen corn, defrost in a sieve.) Take the corn,
onion and all the oil in the pan, and the cheese and add to the
dry ingredients. Fold this gently into the milk mixture until well
blended. Spoon mixture into the well oiled trays until they are
three-quarters full. Bake in the preheated oven for 10 minutes
turning heat down to 200°c/400°F/Gas Mark 6 for a further 6 to
10 minutes until golden and firm on top.

Serve hot spread with butter or polyunsaturated margarine.

Tofu Tempura

Have all the ingredients prepared and coat and fry the tempura just before serving with the Sweet and Sour Sauce (page 80).

700g (1½ lbs) firm tofu, cut into 2.5cm (1 in) chunks
5 tbsps shoyu (naturally fermented soya sauce)
5 tbsps water
small bowl of gram flour (chick pea flour)

Mix shoyu and water together. Put half the shoyu and water into a wide shallow dish, add the tofu cubes then sprinkle the rest of the shoyu and water over the top. Marinate until you are ready to fry, turning the cubes occasionally to coat all sides. Make the batter.

THE BATTER:
170g (6 oz) gram flour (chick pea flour)
50g (2 oz) soya flour
50g (2 oz) brown rice flour
1 rounded tsp baking powder
1 tsp sea salt
575ml (1 pint) water
soya oil for deep frying

Sieve flours, baking powder and sea salt into a mixing bowl, stir in half the water and blend together until smooth and thick. Gradually add the rest of the water and blend until all the lumps are gone and the mixture is a medium, thinnish smooth batter. If using a blender simply put all the ingredients into the blender bowl and process until smooth. Allow to stand for at least 30 minutes while you make the Sweet and Sour Sauce.

When ready to serve heat the oil in a large, heavy-based saucepan to hot (as you would for chips). Using a fork, take the pieces of tofu out of the marinade, roll in the flour then dip into the batter, (by using a fork the excess batter will drip off) and deep fry in 4 batches until golden brown. Drain on absorbent kitchen paper. Place in a large serving dish and pour over the Sweet and Sour Sauce.

Sweet and Sour Sauce

Use sesame oil to give this delicious sauce an authentic taste.
I use less sweetener and less soya sauce than most traditional
recipes and I think the result has a much better and more
subtle flavour.

4 tbsps cold-pressed sesame
   seed oil (sunflower oil will do)
2 medium size onions, finely
   chopped
3 cloves garlic, crushed
2 medium size carrots, scraped
   and very thinly sliced in
   slanting ovals
1 small can bamboo shoots,
   drained and thinly sliced
1 medium size green pepper,
   deseeded and cut in thin rings
   then cut in small slanting
   strips
1 rounded tsp freshly grated
   ginger root

½ level tsp five spice
225g (8 oz) canned pineapple in
   natural juice, drained and
   chopped
4 tbsps of the natural juice from
   the canned pineapple
1 level tbsp clear honey
2 tbsps shoyu (naturally
   fermented soya sauce)
2 tbsps fruit vinegar (see page
   14), cider or wine vinegar
3 tbsps dry sherry
2 tbsps tomato purée
1½ tbsps arrowroot
425ml (15 fl oz) water

Heat the sesame seed oil in a large heavy-based frying pan or
wok and stir-fry the onions, garlic, carrots and bamboo shoots
for 4 minutes only. Add the peppers and continue to stir-fry for a
further 2 minutes. Stir in the grated ginger, five spice and
drained, chopped pineapple. Set aside and mix all the other
ingredients in a mixing bowl adding the water gradually as you
would for a batter. Pour this over the vegetables and cook on a
gentle heat stirring constantly until the mixture thickens. If too
thick then add a little more water. When ready to serve pour
over the Tofu Tempura (page 79).

Baked Rice and Mushrooms

5 tbsps cold-pressed sunflower
  or olive oil
350g (12 oz) small onions, cut
  in thin rings (weight when
  peeled)
350g (12 oz) Surinam long
  grain brown rice
1 level tsp coriander seeds,
  ground
2 cardamom pods, opened and
  seeds crushed
½ tsp black mustard seeds,
  crushed

1 bay leaf
1 tbsp vegetable bouillon
  powder
boiling water
50g (2 oz) blanched almonds
350g (12 oz) small button
  mushrooms
sprinkling of vegetable bouillon
  powder
freshly ground black pepper
1 tbsp lemon juice
2 tbsps chopped coriander
  leaves or parsley

Heat 2 tablespoons of the oil in a medium size heavy-based saucepan and sauté the onions until golden brown. Make a well in the middle, add the spices and bay leaf. When the mustard seeds begin to pop add 1 tablespoon of oil and the rice and cook, stirring the mixture, for 3 further minutes. Pour on the boiling water, and the tablespoon of vegetable bouillon powder, simmer with the lid on for 20 minutes. Remove bay leaf.

While the rice is cooking sauté the mushrooms briskly in 2 tablespoons of the oil for 3 minutes. Add the sprinkling of vegetable bouillon powder, freshly ground black pepper, lemon juice, coriander or parsley and cook on a high heat stirring constantly for a further minute.

Spoon the rice mixture into an ovenproof dish, sprinkle it with half the almonds. Spoon on the mushrooms and their cooking juices, then top with the remaining almonds. Bake uncovered for 10 minutes at 180°c/350°F/Gas Mark 4 until the liquid from the rice has evaporated.

Alfalfa, Orange, Onion and Tomato Salad

Sprouted seeds make wonderful salads in winter (see page 12 on how to sprout these).

175g (6 oz) sprouted alfalfa seeds (weight when sprouted)
6 medium oranges, peeled and diagonally sliced in thin rings
3 small onions, peeled and thinly sliced in rings
8 medium size tomatoes, thinly sliced in rings
2 tbsps fresh parsley, chopped

DRESSING:
3 tbsps cold-pressed olive or sunflower oil
1½ tbsps lime juice
½ level tsp sea salt
freshly ground black pepper
1 small clove garlic, crushed
½ tsp clear honey
½ tsp Dijon mustard
½ tsp dried tarragon

Arrange the sprouted alfalfa in a shallow serving dish. Place oranges, onion and tomatoes overlapping in circles on top of the alfalfa and sprinkle on the parsley.

Shake the dressing ingredients well in a screw-top jar and pour over the salad.

Brandied Winter Fruit and Nut Salad

225g (8 oz) dried apricots
225g (8 oz) stoned prunes
50g (2 oz) dried apple rings, cut in half
110g (4 oz) dried pears, cut in half
50g (2 oz) raisins
2 sticks cinnamon
3 cardamoms, leave whole

¼ tsp clove powder
1 tbsp clear honey
juice of 1 large orange
juice of 1 lemon
enough apple juice to cover fruit
3 tbsps brandy
50g (2 oz) each of slivered almonds, pistachio nuts cut in half and pine nuts

Place all the ingredients except the brandy and nuts in a large saucepan. Pour on enough apple juice to cover and bring to the boil. Transfer to a large bowl, stir in the brandy, cover and leave to marinate overnight or longer. Take out the cinnamon sticks and cardamom seeds. Stir in the nuts, saving a few to sprinkle on the top.

Serve with Greek plain yoghurt if you wish.

Winter Menu for Vegans

Replace the Corn, Cheese and Garlic Sticks (page 78) by the following recipe.

Corn and Garlic Sticks
_____ Makes 14 _____

Follow the recipe for Corn, Cheese and Garlic Sticks (page 78) but omit the cheese, egg and ordinary milk and use 300ml (½ pint) of soya milk instead. Method and baking time remain the same.

The rest of the menu remains the same.

Winter Menu for Meat Lovers

Instead of Tofu Tempura (page 79) do the following recipe.

Fish or Meat Tempura
You can use a variety of fish such as fillet of plaice, lemon sole, or salmon trout (my favourite) and filleted meat such as lamb, turkey, chicken or rabbit. Whichever you use you will need 700g (1½ lbs) in weight when filleted. Cut the flesh into 2.5cm (1 in) wide and 1.25cm (½ in) thick pieces. If using fish, sprinkle with a little sea salt and lemon juice and leave to one side for 1 hour. If using meat then bruise it with a meat tenderiser, rub with a little sea salt, garlic and mixed herbs before dipping in the batter. Use the same batter as for Tofu Tempura (page 79) and deep fry as directed.

The rest of the menu remains the same.

Midsummer Celebration Menu or Wedding Feast

Midsummer is a beautiful time to give a special party such as a 21st birthday celebration or a wedding feast. The gardens and shops abound with a huge variety of fruit and vegetables. Fresh herbs and flowers, both edible and decorative, are more easily available, which helps make creative presentation a delight.

If you are preparing a wedding feast then you won't find a recipe for the traditional ornate, heavily iced wedding cake here. I have instead created a rich fruit cake which could be decorated with crystallized flowers and leaves (see below). Make the cake about 2 months before the party. It will be suitable for any celebration menu.

It is a great help to prepare dishes well beforehand and freeze them, but be careful what you freeze. Fresh is always best. To take the headache out of the last minute rush here is a list of items which you can prepare well in advance.

For the Chick Pea and Sunflower Dip (page 89), freeze the cooked chick peas and 275ml (½ pint) of the cooking liquid in separate containers. Defrost completely and blend with other ingredients as directed.

For the Mushroom and Aubergine Caviar en Croustades (page 90), make and freeze the croustades.

For the Fresh Pea and Herb Barquettes (page 91), make and freeze the barquette pastry cases.

For the Luxury Nut and Seed Loaf (page 92), grind the nuts and freeze. Defrost and mix with other ingredients as directed. (If you pack ground nuts loosely in a polythene bag they will defrost very quickly.)

For the Saffron Rice with Pistachios (page 96), cook rice as directed and freeze loosely in polythene bags. Shell the pistachios and freeze. Defrost completely and add other ingredients as directed.

For the Quartet of Exotic Fruit-Filled Savarins with Passion Fruit and Peach Sauce (page 101), bake and freeze the savarins. Defrost, fill with fruit and pour over sauce on the morning of the event.

Make the Celebration Cake (page 104) 2 months before the event.

Bake and freeze the Nutritious Baguettes (French Loaves) (page 106). To serve, defrost loaves completely, freshen by sprinkling on a little warm water or milk and heat for 10 minutes in the oven, 200°c/ 400°f/Gas Mark 6.

Make the Peach and Apple Chutney (page 107) 1 month before. The flavour improves enormously 2 weeks after potting.

Menu

✿ VEGETARIAN ✿

Crudités
Goat's Cheese with Avocado and Herb Dip
Chick Pea and Sunflower Seed Dip
Mushroom and Aubergine Caviar en Croustades
Fresh Pea and Herb Barquettes
Luxury Nut and Seed Loaf
Asparagus and Tarragon Quiche
Saffron Rice with Pistachios
Tabbouleh (Bulgur Wheat and Pine Kernel Salad)
Potato Salad with Chutney
Paw Paw, Avocado, Mushroom & Chicory Salad with Raspberry Vinaigrette
Herby Green Leaf Salad with Flowers and Lime Vinaigrette
Quartet of Exotic Fruit-Filled Savarins with Passion Fruit and Peach Sauce
Yoghurt Cream
White Wine Summer Fruit Cup
Celebration Cake
Nutritious Baguettes (French Loaves)
Peach and Apple Chutney
Choice of Cheeses

Crudités

These are fresh, raw or lightly cooked vegetables which can be served with a vinaigrette or a dip as a healthy start to any meal. Here is a selection to choose from, but you can of course vary the choice according to season and display them creatively blending colours and textures together.

Raw vegetables to be cut into thin 5cm (2 in) sticks could include: carrots, celery, courgettes, cucumber, green and red peppers. Other whole vegetables such as small spring onions (cut off 5cm (2 in) bulb end and use green stems as you would chives), whole radishes trimmed, red and green chicory leaves and whole small button mushrooms with stalks on so that they can be picked up easily.

Lightly cooked vegetables could include: whole French beans, cauliflower and broccoli florets, very young broad beans cooked in their pods and asparagus tips. To cook, bring water to boil in a medium size saucepan and lightly salt if you wish. Cook French beans for 1 minute, drain (reserve the water), plunge into cold water and drain well. Repeat the process with the other vegetables, cooking separately but using the same water, topping up when necessary. Cauliflower and broccoli will take 1½ minutes to cook, broad beans and asparagus 3 minutes. Arrange creatively and serve with the following two dips.

Goat's Cheese with Avocado and Herb Dip

450g (1 lb) soft goat's curd
cheese
2 good size avocados
1 large juicy clove of garlic,
peeled and crushed
2 tbsps cold-pressed olive oil
2 tbsps fresh squeezed lemon
juice
1 tsp vegetable bouillon powder

1 tbsp fresh basil or marjoram,
chopped (if dried use 1 level
tsp)
2 tbsps finely chopped chives
(or use green stems of spring
onion)
large red pepper
freshly ground black pepper to
taste

Put curd cheese into a mixing bowl. Peel and stone the
avocados (save half of 1 avocado for garnishing and sprinkle it
with lemon juice to stop it browning). Roughly chop the
remaining 1½ avocados and blend with the olive oil, lemon
juice, vegetable bouillon powder, herbs and chives until smooth
and creamy. Stir this into the curd cheese. Cut the red pepper
and deseed saving a quarter for garnish. Chop the rest very
finely and stir into the other ingredients adding freshly ground
pepper to taste. Spoon into a serving bowl.

When ready to serve, cut the avocado half into 8 thin curved
strips lengthwise. Cut the quarter of red pepper in thin curved
strips lengthwise. Arrange these alternately in a circle in the
centre of the dip. Place a sprig of fresh basil or marjoram in the
middle if you have any.

Chick Pea and Sunflower Seed Dip

This is a variation of hummous, which is a Middle Eastern dish traditionally made with purée of chick peas and tahini (sesame seed paste).

450g (1 lb) chick peas (dry
   weight)
1 tsp sea salt
juice of 4 lemons
4 large cloves garlic, peeled and
   crushed
4 tbsps sunflower seed spread

4 tbsps cold-pressed olive oil
1 level tbsp fresh mint, chopped
   (optional but recommended)
sea salt and freshly ground
   black pepper
sprig of mint and cucumber
   slices to garnish

Wash chick peas and pick over for stones. Soak for at least 12 hours changing the water 3 times. Rinse and cook in 2.5 litres (4 pints) of water for about 1 hour until soft, adding 1 teaspoon of sea salt 10 minutes before the end of cooking time. (Do not add salt earlier or the chick peas will not soften.)

Mix lemon juice, garlic, sunflower spread and olive oil together. Now purée the chick peas a quarter at a time with a quarter of the sunflower mixture in a blender until smooth. You may have to add a little of the cooking water to achieve a thick creamy consistency. Spoon into a bowl and stir in the chopped mint and freshly ground black pepper and sea salt to your own taste. Cover and chill until you are ready to serve. Swirl the top and garnish with a circle of overlapping thin slices of cucumber. Ridge down the skin of the cucumber with a curved knife or a fork before slicing to give a pretty serrated edge. Pop a sprig of mint in the centre.

Mushroom and Aubergine Caviar en Croustades

Makes 25

If you would like to serve each guest with one of these delicious tarts then double the recipe. The croustades can be made in advance and frozen. The mushroom and aubergine 'caviar' can be prepared the day before and kept covered in the 'fridge. Fill as near to serving time as possible. Unless your home-baked bread is the right texture – not too dry or too damp and heavy – it is best to use bought sliced wholemeal bread for this recipe and, because you need to cut out 7½cm (3 in) diameter rounds, buy small cut loaves or you will waste too much bread.

CROUSTADES:
25 small slices of wholemeal bread
melted polyunsaturated margarine

FILLING:
12 small dried mushrooms
2 aubergines, approx. 275g (10 oz) each in weight
1 good size green pepper
1 good size red pepper
2 tbsps cold-pressed olive or sunflower oil

1 medium size onion, finely chopped
1 large clove garlic, crushed
¼ tsp cayenne pepper (more if you like)
2 tbsps parsley, finely chopped
2 tbsps lemon juice
1 tbsp tomato pureé

TO GARNISH:
thin strips of red and green pepper
25 black olives, stoned

To make the croustades:
Using a 7.5cm (3 in) round, fluted-edged cutter, cut out 1 round from each slice of bread. Brush on both sides with melted margarine and press into bun tins. Bake in the oven heated to 180°C/350°F/Gas Mark 4 for 20 minutes until deep golden brown. Cool on a wire rack. Freeze if not filling immediately.

To make the filling:
Soak the mushrooms in hot water for 15 minutes. Wash and wipe the aubergines and peppers. Make 3 slits in the aubergines. Heat the grill to maximum for 5 minutes then turn down

to moderate and grill the aubergines and peppers, turning them over continuously until the skins are blistered and charred all over and the flesh is soft. Pop in a colander, rinse in cold water and rub skins off. Pat dry. Roughly chop the aubergines and cut the peppers in half, remove pith and seeds and chop roughly. Sauté the onion and garlic in the oil for 5 minutes. Drain mushrooms, cut off woody stems and discard. Chop the mushroom cups in tiny pieces and sauté with the onions for 5 minutes. Stir in cayenne, parsley, lemon juice and tomato pureé. Put aubergines, peppers and onion mixture into a blender and process until smooth. Cover and chill until ready to fill the croustades.

Garnish with criss-cross strips of red and green pepper and an olive in the centre. Arrange these on a large serving dish in alternate rows with the Fresh Pea and Herb Barquettes.

Fresh Pea and Herb Barquettes
—————————— Makes 25 ——————————

The barquettes (pastry cases) can be made well in advance and frozen. Fill and garnish on the same day as the party. If you wish your guests to have one each then simply double the recipe. Buy lots of barquette moulds and the right cutter. As the pastry has to be very thin I have used wholemeal pastry flour which is very finely milled. I have also used Parmesan cheese but this is not necessary especially if you wish to fill these with a cheesy mixture.

BARQUETTES:
225g (8 oz) wholemeal pastry
  flour
good pinch sea salt
110g (4 oz) cold
  polyunsaturated margarine
3 rounded tbsps Parmesan
  cheese, finely grated
2 tbsps ice-cold water
1 tbsp ice-cold lemon juice
little egg white to brush the
  cases

FILLING:
225g (8 oz) Greek plain yoghurt
1.2kg (2½ lbs) peas in their
  pods (yields about 400g (14
  oz) peas)
¼ tsp freshly ground nutmeg or
  mace
1 level tsp dried tarragon
freshly ground black pepper
little sea salt
very finely chopped parsley to
  garnish (dried is best for this)

For the Barquettes:
Rub the margarine into the flour and salt until it resembles fine crumbs. Stir in the cheese with a fork and sprinkle on the iced water and lemon juice. Blend together using the fork then, with cupped hands, lightly mould together to form a dough. Place in a polythene bag and chill for at least 1 hour. Preheat oven to 200°C/400°F/Gas Mark 6.

Roll out the pastry on a lightly floured surface and cut out boat shapes with the right size cutter. (If you spread a polythene sheet over the pastry when rolling out you will use less flour.) Line the moulds. Now put a piece of foil and a few beans on top of each pastry case. Bake in the preheated oven for 10 minutes. Take out the foil and beans and continue to bake for a further 10 minutes. Allow them to cool completely before removing from the moulds. Freeze if you are not filling the same day. Defrost and fill as near to serving time as possible.

For the filling:
Line a colander with a piece of muslin. Pour in the yoghurt, tie up and let it drip for 4 hours (this separates the curds from the whey and gives you a thick creamy yoghurt cheese). Scrape off the curds from the muslin and leave to one side. Meanwhile, pod the peas and put into boiling water and cook for just 3 minutes or until soft. Drain and immediately plunge into cold water. Leave for 2 minutes then drain well. Take out 25 peas for garnish. Put remaining peas into a blender, add yoghurt cheese, nutmeg or mace and tarragon. Process until smooth. Scoop out and add freshly ground black pepper and sea salt to taste. Chill.

When ready to serve, spoon into the cooked barquette cases. Place one pea in the centre of each and carefully drizzle the parsley first in a thin circle around each pea and then in four lines starting at the edge of the circle to either end and sides of the boat shape.

Luxury Nut and Seed Loaf

This delicious bake can be eaten hot as a main dish accompanied by gravy, roast potatoes and steamed vegetables or cold with cranberry and apple sauce and salad. You would have to cut the recipe by half to serve 8 as a main meal.

In this vegetarian menu the loaf takes the place of meat such as turkey or ham. It looks great as a centrepiece garnished with curly endive and thin slices of cucumber and tomatoes. I have used expensive nuts in this recipe but you can omit the pistachios and pine kernels and use more of the others instead, but this mixture has a very special taste.

225g (8 oz) bulgur wheat
330ml (12 fl oz) boiling water
3 tbsps shoyu (naturally fermented soya sauce)
175g (6 oz) pistachio nuts (weight when shelled)
175g (6 oz) pine kernels
225g (8 oz) blanched almonds
175g (6 oz) cashew nuts
110g (4 oz) hazel nuts
110g (4 oz) pumpkin seeds

250g (12 oz) onion, very finely chopped (weight when peeled)
4 tbsps fresh parsley, finely chopped
2 rounded tsps dried lemon thyme
4 large eggs, lightly whisked
4 tbsps cold-pressed sunflower oil
little oil for pouring on roast

Place bulgur in a mixing bowl and pour on the boiling water and shoyu. Cover and let swell for 25 minutes. Grind nuts and seeds to a medium fine crumb consistency as follows. First grind the pistachios with pine kernels, take out 2 tablespoons of this for top of roast. Then grind the cashews with the pumpkin seeds and finally the almonds with the hazels. Mix all together with the bulgur. Stir in the parsley, lemon thyme, onions, eggs and oil and using your hands mould well together. Let the mixture stand while you prepare the tin and foil hood, which you do as follows.

Oil a large baking sheet and line it with greaseproof paper. Form a loaf shape with the nut mixture to about a 10cm (4 in) width (do this on the oiled baking sheet), press firmly together and prick top with a skewer or fork. Pour on a little oil, sprinkle top with the reserved 2 tablespoons of ground pistachio and pine kernels and cap loosely with a foil hood. Bake in the oven, 190°C/375°F/Gas Mark 5, for 40 minutes. Take off hood, baste with the oil in the baking sheet and continue to bake for a further 10 minutes. Place in a large serving dish when cooled, easing off the paper as you do so. Cover with the hood until ready to garnish. This can be covered overnight. Garnish with curly endive and overlapping slices of cucumber and tomato.

Asparagus and Tarragon Quiche

When catering for large numbers buffet style I prefer to make large rectangular or square quiches as these are easier to cut and handle. Make sure that the sides are as deep as the usual round quiche dishes, i.e. 2.5cm (1 in). The ingredients in this recipe will fit a 30cm (12 in) square or a 35 × 25.5cm (14 × 10 in) rectangular ovenproof dish or tin which is 2.5cm (1 in) deep (inside measurement). When cold you will be able to cut approximately 64 reasonable size slices. You can make 2 round quiches with the same ingredients using 24cm (9½ in) dishes.

PASTRY:
175g (6 oz) cold
   polyunsaturated margarine
   (Vitaquell)
350g (12 oz) wholemeal flour
2 tbsps lightly toasted sesame
   seeds
good pinch sea salt (optional)
4 tbsps ice-cold water
2 tsps lemon juice
FILLING:
450g (1 lb) asparagus, fresh or
   frozen
1 medium size onion, very finely
   chopped

8 large eggs
330ml (12 fl oz) skimmed milk
4 rounded tbsps skimmed milk
   powder
4 rounded tbsps Greek plain
   yoghurt
¼ tsp sea salt
¼ level tsp ground mace
¼ level tsp mustard powder
¼ level tsp freshly ground black
   pepper
1 rounded tsp dried tarragon
225g (8 oz) Cheddar or
   Gruyère cheese, grated
little tarragon for topping

To make the pastry:
Put cold margarine into a mixing bowl. Sieve the flour in another bowl and stir in the sesame seeds and salt if using. Add 4 tablespoons of the flour mixture to the margarine, pour in the water and lemon juice. Using a wooden spoon blend well together for 1 minute gradually adding the rest of the flour mixture and using your hands to form a dough when it gets difficult to use the spoon. Knead for 1 minute flouring your hands if necessary. Place in a polythene bag and chill for at least 30 minutes. Roll out on to a lightly floured surface as thinly as possible to whatever shape your dish is. With a palette knife

ease one edge of the pastry up on to the rolling pin, curl it around a little and lift it up from the surface. Line the well oiled dish or tin and press gently into the sides, trim edges. Prick the base all over with a fork. For perfect results freeze for 10 minutes only. Bake blind in a preheated oven, 200°c/400°f/Gas Mark 6 for 10 minutes, turn the oven down to 190°c/375°f/Gas Mark 5 and cook for a further 5 minutes. Cool completely before filling or freeze if not ready to fill the same day.

For the filling:
If using fresh asparagus wash well and trim off woody ends (save these for vegetable stock, see page 153). Steam asparagus in a steamer or colander over a saucepan of boiling water for 7 minutes only. If frozen then steam for only 4 minutes. Cut off 2.5cm (1 in) tips for garnish and chop the stems roughly. Put the stems into a liquidizer or food processor with a little of the milk, blend until smooth then add eggs, milk, milk powder, yoghurt, salt, mace, mustard, pepper and tarragon and blend well together.

Sprinkle approximately 75g (3 oz) of the cheese onto the base of the cooked and cold pastry case. Sprinkle on the finely chopped onion and top this with 75g (3 oz) more of the cheese. Pour in the egg mixture and arrange asparagus tips on top (cutting thick tips in half). Sprinkle on the remaining 50g (2 oz) of cheese and a little more tarragon. Bake in the preheated oven, 190°c/375°f/Gas Mark 5 for 45 minutes or until golden brown and slightly risen in the centre.

Saffron Rice with Pistachios

For best results cook 450g (1 lb) of rice at a time, *so double the recipe for this menu.* Surinam rice which only takes 25 minutes to cook is used for this recipe.

450g (1 lb) Surinam brown rice
3 tbsps cold-pressed sunflower
  oil
350g (12 oz) onion (weight
  when finely chopped)
good pinch saffron (or 1 level
  tsp turmeric)
thin strip of lime peel
1.1 litres (2 pints) hot water
1 level tbsp vegetable bouillon
  powder

225g (8 oz) fresh or frozen peas,
  lightly cooked
110g (4 oz) sweetcorn kernels,
  lightly cooked
110g (4 oz) pistachio nuts,
  weight when shelled
1 tbsp lime juice
1 tbsp shoyu (naturally
  fermented soya sauce)
2 tbsps freshly chopped parsley
  to garnish
2 slices lime to garnish

Spread the rice out on a large tray and pick over for unhusked grains. Wash well by putting in a sieve and letting cold water run through the grains for 1 minute, drain well. Heat oil in a heavy-based saucepan and sauté the onion for 10 minutes until soft and golden (do not burn). Stir in the saffron and rice and cook on low heat stirring constantly to coat the grains well. Add lime peel, hot water and vegetable bouillon powder, bring to boil and simmer with a tight lid on for 25 minutes. Do not disturb the rice while it is simmering. (If the lid is not tight enough cover with foil, then lid.) The rice will absorb all the cooking liquid, but turn into a colander to make sure and leave for 10 minutes to let steam off. Place in a serving bowl and very lightly fork in peas, sweetcorn, most of the nuts, lime juice and shoyu. Garnish with a few of the remaining nuts, finely chopped parsley and the thin slices of lime cut into twists or butterfly shapes.

Tabbouleh
(Bulgur Wheat and Pine Kernel Salad)

This salad is best if marinated in the dressing for 24 hours.
Bulgur swells enormously and the recipe will fill a large
serving bowl.

450g (1 lb) bulgur wheat
boiling water to soak
3 level tsps vegetable bouillon
  powder
6 tbsps cold-pressed olive or
  sunflower oil
4 tbsps fresh lemon juice
½ tsp freshly ground black
  pepper
4 cloves garlic, crushed
8 tbsps parsley, very finely
  chopped

225g (8 oz) spring onions (use
  green ends as well) very finely
  chopped (Spanish onion will
  do)
1 tbsp fresh mint leaves, very
  finely chopped
8 medium tomatoes, cut in thin
  wedges
175g (6 oz) pine nuts (save a
  few for garnishing)
lettuce and mint sprigs to
  garnish

Place bulgur in a large mixing bowl and pour in enough boiling
water to cover by 2.5cm (1 in). Add the vegetable bouillon
powder and stir all together. Cover tightly with foil and allow to
stand for 25 minutes until it becomes cold. Blend oil, lemon
juice, pepper and garlic together. Stir parsley, onions, mint,
tomatoes and pine nuts into the cold bulgur, pour over the oil
dressing and toss lightly with a large, long-handled salad fork.
Cover this and let it stand in a cool place in the 'fridge for 24
hours. Place on a large shallow serving dish, surround with fresh
small lettuce leaves and sprigs of fresh mint or watercress and
top with a few pine nuts.

Potato Salad with Chutney

3kg (5 lbs) small new potatoes
6 tender inside sticks celery (use
   green leaf tops as well),
   chopped
large sprig mint
1 Spanish onion, very finely
   chopped

6 tbsps peach chutney (page
   107)
8 tbsps mayonnaise (page 37)
6 tbsps fresh parsley, chopped
little parsley to garnish

Cook the potatoes in slightly salted water with the mint for about
10 to 15 minutes until cooked but not too soft. Drain and allow
to cool before cutting in half or quarters according to size. When
cold, stir in the other ingredients lightly with a fork and garnish
with a little chopped parsley.

Paw Paw, Avocado, Mushroom & Chicory Salad with Raspberry Vinaigrette

This delightful salad looks absolutely stunning when the raspberry vinaigrette is trickled over the top. Prepare this as near to serving time as possible for a really fresh and effective presentation.

As suggested in the list of preparations the Raspberry Vinaigrette should be made several weeks before. Choose the same size paw paws and avocados.

4 ripe paw paws
4 avocados, ripe but not too soft
lemon juice (to stop fruit browning)
450g (1 lb) small button mushrooms (small as possible), wiped and thinly sliced
6 heads white chicory, washed and leaves separated
1 clove garlic, crushed

2 heads red chicory (radicchio) washed and leaves separated
chives, very finely chopped to garnish
6 tbsps cold-pressed sunflower or olive oil
3 tbsps raspberry vinegar (see recipe for Fruit Vinegar, page 14)
little sea salt and freshly ground black pepper to taste

Slit the avocados in quarters, peel off the skins and discard the stones. Slice in very thin wedges and dip in the lemon juice. Peel skins off paw paws, cut in half and scoop out the seeds, cutting in very thin wedges. Place the sliced mushrooms in the centre of a large shallow serving dish. Arrange the red and white chicory leaves alternately around the edge of the dish, spreading a few of the red leaves to line the dish up to the mushrooms in the centre. Arrange the avocado and paw paw wedges overlapping in circles around the mushrooms. Sprinkle with the chives.

Put oil, raspberry vinegar, garlic, sea salt and freshly ground black pepper into a screw-top jar, shake well and trickle over the salad.

Herby Green Leaf Salad with Flowers and Lime Vinaigrette

This is simple, refreshing and looks very pretty strewn with edible flowers or simply rose petals (unsprayed of course). You can use borage flowers and marigolds, both look lovely set in green salad leaves. Fresh herbs such as marjoram or basil with chives, parsley and a very little fresh mint is a good combination but do not use dried.

4 good hearted crisp lettuces
3 bunches watercress
4 punnets mustard cress (or even better, garden cress)
6 tbsps fresh herbs, finely chopped
borage and marigold flowers to garnish (rose petals will do)

LIME VINAIGRETTE:
6 tbsps cold-pressed sunflower oil

2 tbsps lime juice
1 tbsp fresh squeezed orange juice
1 level tsp herb salt
½ tsp Dijon mustard
½ tsp clear honey
freshly ground black pepper

Wash the lettuces, shake well and dry. If the leaves are not too big then leave whole as they stay fresher. Wash the cress and chop leaving stems on. Put lettuce leaves and cress in a large, deep glass serving bowl. Sprinkle on the fresh chopped herbs.

Shake all dressing ingredients in a screw-top jar.

When ready to serve sprinkle on the dressing and garnish with the flowers of your choice or rose petals.

Quartet of Exotic Fruit Filled Savarins with Passion Fruit & Peach Sauce

❀

The sweet yeasted dough of savarin is usually made with white flour but I have experimented with both 81% wheatmeal and 100% wholemeal flour with excellent results. Use a strong flour which has a high gluten content for easy rising and a lighter texture. I also add 1 25mg soluble vitamin C tablet which also helps the dough to rise quickly.
I arranged these on 4 large bottle-green tiles because I did not have a large enough dish or platter. A silver tray would look stunning.
The ingredients listed will make 2 23cm (9 in) fruit-filled savarins. It is easier to make 2 at a time, *so double the recipe if making 4.*

FOR 2 SAVARIN MOULDS:
450g (1 lb) 81% wheatmeal or 100% wholemeal strong flour
75g (3 oz) fruit sugar
¼ tsp sea salt (optional)
275ml (½ pint) lukewarm milk
1 level tbsp dried yeast
1 25mg soluble vitamin C tablet
4 medium size eggs, beaten
110g (4 oz) melted polyunsaturated margarine

FILLING FOR 2 SAVARINS:
225g (8 oz) lychees, cut in half and stoned
110g (4 oz) dark red cherries, stoned
3 minolas or juicy oranges, peeled and segmented

110g (4 oz) seedless grapes
1 medium size mango, peeled and sliced in small pieces
2 kiwi fruit, peeled and sliced thinly
225g (8 oz) strawberries, hulled and sliced
2 large bananas, sliced
little lemon juice to sprinkle on sliced bananas

PASSION FRUIT AND PEACH SAUCE FOR 2 SAVARINS:
225g (8 oz) very ripe peaches
juice of ½ lime
1 tbsp fruit sugar
3 drops natural vanilla essence
3 passion fruit, peeled
1 tbsp peach brandy (optional)

For the savarins:
Blend flour, sugar and salt together in a large mixing bowl. Make a well in the centre and pour in the lukewarm milk, yeast, vitamin C tablet and beaten eggs. Beat well together until smooth. Add the melted margarine and beat the mixture for

about 2 to 3 minutes. (This is important as you cannot knead this yeasted batter.) Half fill the 2 well greased savarin moulds, cover loosely with a lightly greased polythene bag and leave to rise to the top of the moulds. While rising, set oven to 200°c/400°f/Gas Mark 6. Bake in the centre of the preheated oven for about 20 minutes.

Cool slightly in the tins and then turn out on to a wire rack and continue to cool until lukewarm (about 5 minutes). Turn on to the serving dish and prick with a fork.

While the savarins are cooking prepare the sauce and fruit salad. The sauce must be poured over the lukewarm savarins so the juices are absorbed more easily.

For the filling:
Prepare the fruit as near to serving time as possible. Put all the chopped fruit except the bananas in a bowl. Sprinkle the bananas with lemon juice to prevent them browning and add these to the other fruits.

For the sauce:
Blanch the peaches in hot water for 1 minute, peel, stone and roughly chop. Do this on a plate to retain any juice that might squeeze out as you peel and chop. Cook the peach fruit in a small heavy-based saucepan, with the lime juice, sugar and vanilla for about 4 minutes until soft. Take off heat and add the passion fruit. Purée the mixture in a blender then press through a sieve. Reheat on low temperature. Stir in the brandy if using and pour three quarters of this warm sauce over the lukewarm savarins. These can be left overnight covered loosely, then filled with the freshly prepared fruit as near to serving time as possible. Pour the remaining quarter of the sauce over the fruit in the centre of the savarins. Serve with Yoghurt Cream.

Yoghurt Cream

The following recipe for Yoghurt Cream looks beautiful in a glass or a silver goblet and placed in the centre of the quartet of savarins (see above). You may want to put more into a glass serving bowl. In this recipe I use a little cream but you can just serve the thick yoghurt on its own.

275ml (½ pint) double cream
1 tbsp fruit sugar
900g (2 lbs) Greek plain
   yoghurt

sprinkling of powdered
   cinnamon

Whip cream in a mixing bowl until stiff. Whisk in the sugar and then the yoghurt. Spoon some into the goblet and sprinkle on the cinnamon. Spoon the remainder into a serving bowl, sprinkle on a little more cinnamon and place by the side of the savarins.

White Wine Summer Fruit Cup
—————————— Fills 50 wine glasses ——————————

This delicious and moderately alcoholic drink is very refreshing on a hot summer day. If preparing a wedding feast then traditionally the bride and groom are toasted in champagne. I served this as an alternative to toast my son and his bride and fortunately I had another 5 litres tucked away in the pantry which disappeared as quickly as the first bowl. The colour is of a rosé wine.
This recipe will fill a 6 litre (10½ pint) punch bowl and be enough to give 50 guests one wine glassful each.

450g (1 lb) firm large ripe
   strawberries, hulled and
   sliced
150ml (¼ pint) raspberry juice
   concentrate (sugar-free)
275ml (½ pint) Cointreau
juice of 6 oranges
juice of 3 limes

5 bottles of Hock or Riesling,
   chilled
1 litre (1¾ pints) naturally
   sparkling mineral water
mint, lemon balm, or lemon
   verbena leaves to garnish

Put the sliced strawberries into the punch bowl and pour over the raspberry juice concentrate, Cointreau, orange juice and lime juice. Leave to marinate for 1 hour. Just before the guests arrive add the white wine and sparkling mineral water. The strawberry slices will float to the top. Garnish with a few herb leaves of your choice.

Celebration Cake

This rich fruit mixture makes a wonderful wedding, Christmas, or special occasion cake. If making for a wedding then bake in a heart-shaped tin. What you decorate it with will, of course, have to suit the occasion. Here I have strewn it with flowers and leaves which are preserved in a solution of sugar, egg white and rose water. The flowers will last for up to 2 months so you can choose out-of-season flowers such as primroses and violets which look really beautiful. Small roses or individual rose petals, geraniums and forget-me-nots also make charming decorations. If you wish to ice in the traditional manner then this cake will make a perfect base. If icing, make the cake 3 months before it is required and ice 1 month after storage. If not icing, then make it 2 months before needed and store as directed.

This recipe will fill a 28cm (11 in) round, or a 25cm (10 in) square cake tin. Line the greased tin with 2 layers of greaseproof paper and tie a double thickness of brown paper around the outside of the tin. Have a sheet of brown paper ready folded in four to place under the cake in the oven. Long, slow cooking of this well protected cake, and a long enough storage time, is essential to achieve a perfect cutting texture and full flavour.

3 tbsps brandy
juice and rind of 1 orange
juice and rind of 1 lemon
560g (1¼ lbs) wholemeal flour, plain
1 rounded tsp freshly ground nutmeg
1 level tsp freshly ground allspice
1 level tsp ground cinnamon
½ level tsp clove powder
450g (1 lb) polyunsaturated margarine
225g (8 oz) Barbados sugar
8 large eggs, beaten
350g (12 oz) currants

350g (12 oz) raisins
350g (12 oz) sultanas
175g (6 oz) dried apricots (unsulphured), finely chopped
175g (6 oz) dried pineapple (unsweetened), finely chopped
175g (6 oz) dried papaya (unsweetened), finely chopped
175g (6 oz) glacé cherries, washed, dried and cut in quarters
110g (4 oz) dried apple flakes or rings (if rings, cut in small pieces)
175g (6 oz) pecan nuts, chopped (almonds will do)
little brandy to soak cake after cooking

The day before mix orange rind and juice, lemon rind and juice and brandy together. Store in a screw-top jar. Mix fruit with the nuts. Sieve flour and spices together. Cream margarine and sugar until light and fluffy. Gradually beat in the eggs adding a little flour if the mixture curdles. Gradually fold in the flour alternately with the fruit and nut mixture, (do not beat). Stir in the brandy, orange and lemon mixture. Spoon into the prepared cake tin, level gently using the back of the spoon and then hollow the middle a little or the cake will rise in the centre too much.

Preheat oven, 150°C/300°F/Gas Mark 2 and when correct temperature is reached place cake on top of the folded sheet of brown paper on the bottom shelf of the oven and bake for 5 hours. Turn down heat to 130°C/250°F/Gas Mark ½ and continue to cook for about 2 hours more. The cake will be cooked when a skewer inserted in the centre comes out clean. If the cake is browning too quickly on top place a sheet of greaseproof paper over it. Let it cool in the tin for 1 hour then turn out on to a wire rack. If you like, prick the top in several places with a skewer and trickle on a little brandy. Let it cool completely then wrap in greaseproof paper and store upside down in an airtight tin for 2 months.

To crystallize flowers you will need plenty of caster sugar, but most of it is shaken off. Heat the oven to 100°C/200°F/Gas very low. Beat some egg whites lightly with a fork and add 1 teaspoon rose water for every 1 egg white. Paint the flowers and petals with this mixture. Take care to coat thoroughly and thinly; any uncovered area will go mouldy. Spread a thick layer of sifted caster sugar on a baking tray. Place coated flowers on this and sprinkle them liberally with more sugar. Shake off excess and transfer flowers to a wire rack covered with baking parchment. Dry in the oven for about 24 hours, turning once after 40 minutes. Store in an airtight tin.

With the following 2 recipes for Baguettes (French loaves) and Peach and Apple Chutney, I suggest you have a selection of about 6 different cheeses. For those who wish to buy cheese made with vegetable rennet there is an increasing variety to choose from in health shops and some supermarkets.

I usually set the cheese board aside on a separate table with a large basket of baguettes, several bowls of chutney and the coffee cups ready to fill.

Nutritious Baguettes (French Loaves)

I rarely make bread with as much unbleached white flour as
in these loaves but the combination here is a healthier
alternative to the usual all white French loaf.

This recipe will make 6 340g (12 oz) loaves. Make 18 and
you will have plenty for 50 guests. They freeze well so you
can make them in 3 batches well before the party. As
suggested in the introduction to this menu, if frozen let them
defrost completely, sprinkle on a little water and warm in the
oven for 10 minutes, 190°C/375°F/Gas Mark 5. You will need
2 large baking sheets approximately 30 × 35cm (12 × 14 in)
greased and floured.

450g (1 lb) wholemeal flour
275ml (½ pint) milk, lukewarm
1 egg, beaten
2 tbsps cold-pressed sunflower
 oil
25g (1 oz) dried yeast
575ml (1 pint) water, lukewarm
1 dessertspoon fruit sugar

790g (1¾ lbs) unbleached
 white flour
110g (4 oz) full fat soya flour
1 rounded tsp sea salt (optional)
few sesame seeds to top
little warm water with a pinch of
 sea salt

Place wholemeal flour in a large mixing bowl and with a
wooden spoon stir in the milk, 275ml (½ pint) of the lukewarm
water, the egg and the oil. Mix to a batter consistency. Dissolve
the yeast in the remaining 275ml (½ pint) water. Stir in the
sugar and leave in a warm place to froth for about 5 minutes.
When frothy stir into the batter mixture and beat lightly for 1
minute, enfolding plenty of air. Sieve unbleached white flour,
soya flour and sea salt together and add this gradually to the
batter mixture using your hands when it gets too stiff to blend.
Work this into a soft dough kneading well together while still in
the bowl. If a little sticky then add more flour. Turn out on to a
work surface and knead for 5 minutes more. Place dough in a
large greased polythene bag, press out the air and secure the
top with a wire tie. Wrap loosely in a large warm towel and let it
rise in a warm place until doubled in size.

Before breaking the dough into 6 equal portions, knead for 2
minutes. Put 5 portions back in the polythene bag (not

touching) and roll out the first portion to an oval shape approximately 20 × 10cm (8 × 4 in). Roll this up as you would a Swiss roll and press gently into a French loaf shape about 30cm (12 in) long. Place this on the greased baking sheet. Repeat with the rest of the dough. Cover the 2 trays by sliding them into 2 large polythene bags making sure there is enough room for the loaves to double in size.

Preheat oven at this stage to 220°C/425°F/Gas Mark 7. Pour 2.5cm (1 in) boiling water into a roasting tin and place on the floor of the oven. When loaves have risen, cut 4 shallow diagonal slits on the top of each, brush with the warm water and salt and sprinkle on a few sesame seeds. Bake on 2 shelves, one in the centre of the oven and the other just above, for 8 minutes. Turn trays around and continue to bake for another 7 minutes. Sprinkle on a little warm water after 8 minutes as this crispens the crust. Cool on a wire rack.

If freezing then let the loaves cool completely first (see page 106 for defrosting and reheating).

Peach and Apple Chutney
—————— Makes 7 450g (1 lb) jars ——————

You can use fresh peaches for this but you will need 1.4kg (3 lbs) instead of 450g (1 lb) dried peaches. If using fresh then follow same method but skin the peaches before stoning and chopping by blanching in boiling water for half a minute. Cooking time for fresh peaches is 20 minutes. This recipe uses dried unsulphured peaches which means that you can make this well in advance. The tablespoon of cayenne pepper seems a lot but the chutney is not hot.

450g (1 lb) dried unsulphured
   peaches
425ml (¾ pint) cider vinegar
350g (12 oz) demerara sugar
1 large green pepper, deseeded
   and chopped
1 large red pepper, deseeded
   and chopped
3 large cooking apples, peeled
   and chopped

175g (6 oz) raisins or sultanas
1 level tbsp cayenne pepper
2 tbsps freshly grated ginger
   root
1 level dessertspoon freshly
   ground coriander
1 tbsp white mustard seeds
6 large cloves garlic, peeled and
   crushed

Wash the peaches by pouring boiling water over them. Rinse, drain and soak in cold water for 24 hours. Drain and chop each into quarters. (Soaking liquid not needed for the recipe.) Put vinegar and sugar into a large saucepan and put on a low heat to melt the sugar. Add all other ingredients, stir well and bring to boil. Simmer with the lid on for 30 minutes. Spoon the hot chutney into warm sterilized preserving jars. You can try a little the next day but the flavour improves after 2 weeks.

Midsummer Celebration Menu or Wedding Feast Menu for Vegans

You will find that I have used tofu wherever possible in those dishes which require cheese. Some recipes I have changed completely but the end result is still a beautiful spread.

Instead of Goat's Cheese and Avocado Dip (page 88) do the following recipe.

Tofu and Avocado Dip
Follow the recipe for Goat's Cheese and Avocado Dip (page 88) but use 450g (1 lb) tofu instead of the goat's cheese.

Instead of the recipe for Fresh Pea and Herb Barquettes (page 91) do:

Fresh Pea, Smoked Tofu and Herb Barquettes
Follow the recipe for Fresh Pea and Herb Barquettes but omit the Parmesan cheese from the pastry and substitute 110g (4 oz) smoked tofu for the yoghurt in the filling. The smoked tofu will give you that extra flavour which you lose without the Parmesan cheese and yoghurt.

In the recipe for the Luxury Nut and Seed Loaf (page 92) simply omit the eggs and blend 2 rounded tablespoons of buckwheat flour with a little water and stir into the mixture. Follow the instructions in the vegetarian menu.

Instead of the Asparagus and Tarragon Quiche (page 94) do the following recipe which has a tofu and asparagus filling and is quite delicious. I have made it into a pie with a pastry topping because the tofu gets too dry if baked open-topped as you would a quiche. Roll the pastry out as thinly as possible. I have given you plenty of dough to play with so if you have any left over after trimming, freeze it and use for vegie pasties later.

The pie looks great if you decorate it with asparagus tip shapes made from pastry trimmings. Arrange them around a circle in the middle or just in the centre. When available use leeks instead of onion in this recipe.

Asparagus, Tomato, Tarragon and Tofu Pie

PASTRY:

Double the pastry recipe for Asparagus and Tarragon Quiche (page 94) and use soya milk for brushing the top.

FILLING:

450g (1 lb) asparagus, fresh or frozen (trimmed weight)

2 tbsps cold-pressed sunflower oil

1 large Spanish onion, very finely chopped

1 large clove garlic, crushed

½ tsp ground mace

½ tsp ground mustard powder

1 level tbsp arrowroot

2 tsps dried tarragon

700g (1½ lbs) firm tofu

1 tbsp vegetable bouillon powder

freshly ground black pepper to taste

6 ripe firm tomatoes, cut in 5 thin slices each, then halved

little more dried tarragon

If using fresh asparagus then wash well and trim off woody ends. Steam asparagus for 7 minutes only. If using frozen, 4 minutes steaming will be sufficient. Cut off the tips and reserve, chop the stems in small pieces and leave to cool. Sauté the onion and garlic in the oil for about 10 minutes until soft. In a blender or food processor put mace, mustard, arrowroot, tarragon, tofu, vegetable bouillon powder and asparagus stems, processing until smooth. Scoop out and stir into the onion and garlic adding the freshly ground black pepper to your taste. Spread this mixture into the baked pastry base. Slice the tips in half and dot all over the filling pressing them gently in. Arrange the tomato half-slices on top pressing these into the filling so that they still show. Roll out remaining pastry and cover the top, sealing the edges with a little water or soya milk. Crimp the edges, or decorate with the asparagus-shaped pastry trimmings around the edges and in the centre. Brush the pastry with a little soya milk and bake in a preheated oven, 190°c/375°f/Gas Mark 5, for 30 minutes.

In the recipe for Potato Salad with Chutney (page 98) omit the mayonnaise and mix the chutney with lime vinaigrette (page 100) and stir this into the potato salad.

Instead of the Quartet of Exotic Fruit Filled Savarins (page 101) offer an exotic fruit salad bowl for which you will need 4 times the fruit filling used in the savarins and double the recipe for Peach Sauce.
  Serve with Sesame and Ginger Snaps (page 137).

The Celebration Cake (page 104) can easily be made without eggs but keep the top covered loosely with a sheet of greaseproof paper during the cooking time.

For the Nutritious Baguettes (page 106) use soya milk or all water and omit the egg. They still turn out light and delicious.

The rest of the menu remains the same.

Midsummer Celebration Menu or Wedding Feast Menu for Meat Lovers

Omit the Luxury Nut and Seed Loaf (page 92) and do the following recipe for Turkey, Chestnut and Vegetable Terrine. The quantity of meat you will use for this recipe is about one third of the meat you would require to serve the turkey in slices to 50 guests. The contrast of colours created with the spinach and red pepper layers looks stunning and appetizing.
  A 3.5kg (approximately 8 lbs) free-range turkey will give you just under 2 kg (4 lbs) of meat. (You can use 2 1.8kg (4 lbs) free-range chickens and prepare in the same way as for the turkey.) See notes on free-range meat (page 21).
  You will need 2 1.7 litre (3 pint) capacity rectangular terrine dishes.

Turkey, Chestnut and Vegetable Terrine

TURKEY STOCK POT:

1 3.5kg (approx. 8 lb) free-
 range turkey
1.7 litres (3 pints) vegetable
 bouillon powder
4 outside sticks celery, chopped
 (use green leafy tops as well)
4 medium carrots, chopped
2 large Spanish onions,
 chopped
2 bay leaves
12 black peppercorns
12 whole coriander seeds

CHESTNUT STUFFING PURÉE:

225g (8 oz) dried chestnuts
little turkey stock liquid
12 small dried mushrooms
2 tbsps cold-pressed sunflower
 oil
1 onion, finely chopped (about
 175g (6 oz) when peeled)
turkey heart and liver, finely
 chopped

110g (4 oz) lean green bacon,
 minced
2 tbsps parsley, chopped
1 heaped tsp dried sage
50g (2 oz) wholemeal
 breadcrumbs, lightly toasted
sea salt and freshly ground
 black pepper to taste

VEGETABLE LAYERS:

700g (1½ lbs) spinach (tough
 stalks removed)
450g (1 lb) sweet red peppers

JELLY LIQUID:

1 litre (1¾ pints) turkey stock
 liquid
150ml (¼ pint) dry white wine
2 tbsps lemon juice
12 leaves gelatine or 40g (just
 under 2 oz) powdered
 gelatine

GARNISH:

flat-leafed parsley sprigs and a
 few fresh sage leaves

For the turkey stock pot:
Get your butcher or supplier to cut the turkey into 6 joints.
(Reserve the heart and liver for the stuffing.) Put the joints into a
large heavy-based saucepan, add all the other ingredients for
the turkey stock pot and bring to the boil; turn down to simmer
with the lid on for about 45 minutes or until the meat is tender.
Allow to cool in the stock for at least 2½ hours then remove the
turkey joints. Strain the stock through a muslin-lined sieve, do
not press through, let it drip. Allow it to stand before skimming
off the fat. Pour through another muslin-lined sieve and reserve
the stock for the jelly.
 First cut the white meat off the bone into medium size pieces,

then the darker meat, keeping the white and dark meat separate. Cover while you prepare the stuffing and vegetables.

For the chestnut stuffing purée:
Soak the chestnuts overnight. Cook in slightly salted water for 1 hour (do this while the turkey is cooking). Soak the mushrooms in hot water for 15 minutes then chop off and discard woody stalks. Chop the mushrooms into small pieces. Sauté the onion, mushrooms, heart, liver and bacon in the oil for about 7 minutes. Crumble the chestnuts and add to the pan with the parsley and sage. Cook for a further 3 minutes on a gentle heat. Blend the lot in a blender or food processor until thick, medium smooth and spreadable. Scoop into a bowl and add a few toasted breadcrumbs to thicken if necessary. Add sea salt and pepper to taste.

For the vegetable layers:
Blanch the spinach in boiling water for 2 minutes, do not cook. Drain and cool in iced cold water. Drain and pat dry. Deseed the peppers but leave them whole, cover with boiling water and cook rapidly for just 1½ minutes. Drain well and finely slice.

For the jelly:
Measure out 1 litre (1¾ pints) of turkey stock liquid. Dissolve the gelatine leaves or powder in 270ml (½ pint) of the stock over very gentle heat. Take off heat and immediately stir in the rest of the stock, white wine and lemon juice, taste and add a little sea salt if necessary. Chill until the consistency of unbeaten egg white (thickish but still runny).

Arrange the terrine layers as follows, remembering that the bottom layer in the dish will be your top layer when it is turned out.
Layer 1: Arrange 3 sprigs of flat-leaf parsley and a few sage leaves on the bottom of both dishes, pour on a little of the jelling liquid then spread white turkey meat on top taking care not to move the herbs.
Layer 2: Use half the stuffing and spread this over the turkey pieces, i.e. a quarter of the stuffing in each dish.
Layer 3: Use all the well drained spinach leaves and divide equally to spread over the stuffing.
Layer 4: Arrange white turkey meat all around the edge of both terrine dishes and the darker meat in the centre.

Layer 5: Use the other half of the stuffing, divide between the 2 dishes and spread this over the turkey.

Layer 6: Divide the chopped peppers equally and spread a layer in each dish.

Layer 7: Arrange white turkey meat all around the edge of the dish and fill the centre with darker meat.

Finally, pour equal quantities of the chilled jelly mixture into each terrine and chill until set.

Turn out on to serving dishes and surround with a few flat-leafed parsley sprigs and sage leaves. The top of the terrine will picture, under the jelly, the leaves which were placed under the turkey and vegetable layers.

The rest of the menu remains the same.

Some International Menus

ITALY

I have very fond memories of dining out in Italy's friendly restaurants. I suppose the fact that my small children were not only accepted with open arms, but invariably whisked away into the kitchens, given loving embraces and stuffed with secret treats much to their delight, helped me to appreciate the food, as I could relax and eat it without having to keep the children quiet. In most restaurants elsewhere children are considered a nuisance, half portions are frowned upon and any exuberant natural behaviour is expected to be repressed immediately.

In those days, although I had no aspirations to be a cookery writer, I loved cooking and usually ended up in the restaurant kitchens nosing into the bubbling saucepans and scribbling down recipes on bus tickets, road maps or the back of my hand. It was there, exactly 22 years ago that I was given a present of my first fresh basil, oregano and tarragon herbs. Previously I had used only fresh parsley, a few sprigs of mint, thyme and sage and dried herbs. I can still remember the thrill that the smell of these three plants gave me. The chef of the hotel we were staying in dug them up with great care, potted them and presented them with instructions on how to look after them, saying that without these his beautiful sauces would taste ordinary. Herbs play as important a part in Italian cooking as spices do in Indian cuisine.

Parmesan, which is used extensively throughout Italy, is a hard, sharp-tasting cheese which when freshly grated adds a wonderful richness to soups, sprinkled on baked dishes and over pasta sauces. A very similar cheese available in the Roman region is Pecorino. It is made from ewe's milk and I think it is even tastier than Parmesan. You can buy it in some well stocked delicatessens and it is about half the price.

Ricotta cheese is also made from ewe's milk. It is a soft cheese and very low in fat. It can be used in making cheese cakes or mixed with a little honey and served with fruit instead of cream. You can also add it to a basic white sauce to enrich the flavour as I have done in the batter sauce to top the Vegetable Lasagne in this menu.

The most widely used ingredients of all are pasta and cold-pressed (virgin) olive oil (see page 14 for more information on olive oil). In moderation pasta, if made with wholemeal or a mixture of wheatmeal and buckwheat or soya flour is not fattening and is a highly nutritious, well balanced food rich in protein, vitamins, minerals and fibre. So, enjoy the delicious lasagne in this menu and have a go at making your own pasta (see pages 18–19).

❀   VEGETARIAN   ❀

Celeriac, Red Pepper and Hazelnut Chicory Boats
Vegetable and Almond Lasagne Verdi
Steamed Broccoli with Artichoke Hearts and
Peppermint
Chestnut and Chocolate (or Carob) Ice Cream
Apricot Sauce

Celeriac, Red Pepper and Hazelnut Chicory Boats

The quantities given below will give you a large platter of stuffed chicory leaves and a refreshing starter before the rich lasagne dish. You can prepare the boats a few hours before serving. You can now buy hazelnut spread which is absolutely delicious and is made in the same way as peanut butter. Try to obtain fresh basil.

2 medium size celeriac roots, peeled
2 small red peppers, deseeded and finely chopped
2 tbsps chopped chives or spring onions
4 tbsps cold-pressed olive or sunflower oil
1 rounded tbsp hazelnut spread
2 tbsps lemon juice

1 level tsp dried tarragon
2 tbsps fresh basil, chopped (optional) or 2 level tsps dried
1 level tsp Dijon mustard
1 level tsp clear honey
2 rounded tbsps Greek plain yoghurt
sea salt and freshly ground black pepper
4 heads of white chicory, washed and leaves separated
sprinkling of dried tarragon to garnish

Grate the celeriac on the largest grating holes and mix with the red peppers and chives or spring onions. Blend oil, hazelnut spread, lemon juice, tarragon, basil, mustard, honey, sea salt and pepper well together. (Best results are achieved in a liquidizer.) Stir in the yoghurt and pour over the celeriac mixture, leaving this to marinate for 1 hour.

When ready to serve spread the chicory leaves in a serving dish and spoon in the salad mixture. Sprinkle over a little dried tarragon.

Note: If you have fresh basil then garnish with a few sprigs.

Vegetable and Almond Lasagne Verdi

Makes 16 portions

You will need 2 25cm (10 in) square baking dishes. You can use bought pasta either the pre-cooked or ordinary dried variety, but the final dish is superior using homemade lasagne verdi (see page 19 for the recipe). Pasta for lasagne, cannelloni and ravioli are the easiest to make especially if you haven't a pasta machine. Traditionally lasagne is made with meat as an ingredient but I have made it with vegetables and a cheese sauce as in this recipe; with vegetables and tofu (page 122) and with lamb and bacon (page 124). Each proved to be a great success.

Use freshly grated Parmesan cheese if possible as the commercially packaged grated Parmesan varies enormously in quality and flavour.

Instead of the traditional béchamel sauce to top the dish I have given you a much simpler batter sauce (it means one less saucepan to wash up!)

450g (1 lb) homemade pasta verdi (page 19)

4 tbsps cold-pressed olive or sunflower oil

2 large onions, about 450g (1 lb) in weight when peeled and chopped

3 large cloves garlic, peeled and crushed

1 good size celery heart, finely chopped

4 medium size courgettes, finely chopped

2 medium size green peppers, deseeded and chopped

225g (8 oz) small button mushrooms, sliced

2 large bay leaves

2 tbsps fresh basil, chopped, or 2 rounded tsps dried

4 tbsps fresh parsley, chopped

2 sprigs fresh thyme, chopped, or ½ tsp dried

175g (6 oz) almonds, roughly chopped

3 400g (14 oz) cans tomatoes, chopped with juice

2 heaped tbsps tomato purée

vegetable bouillon powder

1 wine glass of red wine

freshly ground black pepper

BATTER SAUCE AND CHEESE TOPPING:

570ml (1 pint) milk

225g (8 oz) ricotta cheese or 275ml (½ pint) natural yoghurt

½ tsp ground mace

3 eggs

1½ tbsps soya flour

1½ tbsps unbleached white flour

little sea salt and freshly ground
   black pepper
175g (6 oz) freshly grated
   Parmesan cheese

2 level tsps dried oregano or
   marjoram

If making your own pasta verdi, follow the directions on page 19, rest the dough and roll it out as thinly as possible. To fill the 2 dishes with 3 layers of pasta you will need 48 lasagne sheets each measuring approximately 13 × 6cm (5 × 2½ in). Break dough into four, keeping the other portions of dough in the polythene bag while you roll out one lump at a time. Roll one piece to a 38cm × 25.5cm (15 in × 10 in) rectangular shape and cut this into 8 equal rectangles. Spread these on to lightly floured kitchen paper while you make the vegetable filling (40 minutes).

To make the vegetable filling:
Heat the oil in a large frying pan and sauté the onions and garlic for 5 minutes. Add the celery and courgettes and fry for a further 3 minutes. Add the peppers, mushrooms, bay leaf, basil, parsley, thyme and almonds and continue to fry for another 3 minutes, stirring ingredients from time to time. Stir in the chopped tomatoes, purée, vegetable bouillon powder, red wine and freshly ground black pepper. Cook with the lid off for 10 minutes to evaporate some of the juice.

To make the batter sauce and topping simply put all the ingredients and 2 tablespoons of the Parmesan into a blender and process until smooth.

Now cook your pasta. Bring a large saucepan of water, lightly salted, to boil and ease in the pasta sheet by sheet. Let the water remain boiling and cook the pasta for 5 minutes if homemade, or follow the directions on the packet for bought pasta. When cooked lay out the strips on a clean sealed or formica top. Grease your ovenproof dishes and place 8 sheets of pasta on the base of each. Spoon over half of the vegetable filling between the 2 dishes. Cover each with 8 more pasta sheets, share the rest of the vegetable filling between the 2 dishes and cover with the remaining pasta sheets.

Pour over the batter sauce and sprinkle on the remaining Parmesan cheese dividing both equally. Finally, sprinkle on a little dried oregano or majoram and bake, 180°c/350°F/Gas Mark 4 for 35 to 40 minutes.

Steamed Broccoli with Artichoke Hearts & Peppermint

900g (2 lbs) broccoli florets
395g (14 oz) can artichoke
   hearts

little polyunsaturated margarine
1 tbsp fresh peppermint leaves,
   finely chopped or a little dried

Just before serving steam the broccoli for about 6 minutes until tender but not soggy. Slice the artichoke hearts into quarters and add these to the broccoli 2 minutes before the end of steaming time.

Transfer to a warm serving dish, dot with a little poly-unsaturated margarine and sprinkle on the chopped peppermint.

Chestnut and Chocolate (or Carob) Ice Cream

Here I have almost thrown care to the winds, but I salve my conscience by using quark instead of double cream which is used in the traditional recipe, and pure maple syrup instead of sugar. You can make this well in advance and take out of the freezer 30 minutes before serving. This recipe fills a 1.7 litre (3 pint) ice cream mould. Decorate it with hibiscus or borage flowers if in season and a few sprigs of lemon balm or mint.

175g (6 oz) bitter chocolate or
   carob bar, chopped (see page
   24 for information on carob)
4 tbsps pure maple syrup
225g (8 oz) canned chestnut
   purée (usually lightly
   sweetened)

700g (1½ lb) quark (see page
   16)
2 tbsps Kirsch
3 egg whites
225g (8 oz) whole canned
   chestnuts in syrup, drained
   (save a few for decoration)

Melt the chocolate in the maple syrup in a saucepan over a pan of hot water. Blend well together and stir into the chestnut purée. Beat in the quark and Kirsch. Whisk the egg whites until stiff and fold into the mixture. Freeze this for 2 hours in a shallow tray covered with foil. Scrape out and blend in a mixer until smooth. Put into a mixing bowl and stir in the chopped chestnuts. Spoon into the mould, cover and freeze until 30 minutes before serving. Loosen from the mould by slipping into hot water. Turn out on to a serving dish and decorate with the reserved chestnuts cut in half and the flowers and leaves if you have any.

Apricot Sauce

You can make this simple sauce with fresh apricots and apple juice concentrate or canned apricots in their own juice (unsweetened). The recipe will be enough for pouring a little over 10 servings of ice cream.

450g (1 lb) fresh ripe apricots   *2 tbsps or more of apple juice concentrate*

Blanch the apricots in boiling water for 30 seconds. Peel and stone then blend with the apple juice concentrate until you have a smooth runny purée.

   If using canned, simply purée the apricots gradually adding the unsweetened juice from the can to achieve a runny purée consistency. Serve separately with the Chestnut and Chocolate (or Carob) Ice Cream.

Italian Menu for Vegans

In the recipe for Celeriac, Red Pepper and Hazelnut Chicory Boats (page 117) omit the yoghurt and use more lemon juice to your taste.

Instead of the Vegetable and Almond Lasagne Verdi (page 118) do the following recipe.

Vegetable and Tofu Lasagne Verdi

Use the recipe for 450g (1 lb) pasta verdi for vegans (page 19). Follow the ingredients and method in the recipe for Vegetable and Almond Lasagne Verdi up until the batter sauce and cheese topping and do this tofu sauce and nut topping instead.

570ml (1 pint) soya milk
3 rounded tbsps soya flour
½ tsp ground mace
½ tsp sea salt and freshly
  ground black pepper
225g (8 oz) firm tofu, broken up

110g (4 oz) roughly ground
  pistachio nuts or almonds
1 rounded tsp vegetable
  bouillon powder
2 level tsps dried oregano

Blend the milk, flour, mace, sea salt and freshly ground black pepper in a liquidizer or food processor until smooth. Bring to boil on low heat stirring constantly and cook for 1 minute. Pour into the blender and add the tofu, process until smooth. Pour over the filled lasagne. Mix nuts, vegetable bouillon powder and oregano together and sprinkle over the tofu sauce. Bake at 200°C/400°F/Gas Mark 6 for 20 minutes only.

Instead of the Chestnut and Chocolate (or Carob) Ice Cream (page 120) do the following recipe which is much simpler and a lovely dessert. This is very rich so give only small portions.

Chestnut and Chocolate (or Carob) Cream Jelly

900ml (1½ pints) soya milk
3 tsps agar-agar
175g (6 oz) bitter chocolate or
  carob bar, broken up
4 tbsps maple syrup
few drops vanilla essence

225g (8 oz) canned chestnut
  purée
2 tbsps Kirsch or Grand Marnier
225g (8 oz) whole canned
  chestnuts in syrup, drained
little grated chocolate or carob
  bar to garnish

Heat the milk to warm and stir in the agar-agar. Boil and keep stirring until the agar-agar dissolves completely. Remove from heat. Melt the chocolate or carob bar in the maple syrup in a saucepan over a pan of hot water. When completely melted stir well and pour this into the hot milk mixture. Whisk in the vanilla essence, chestnut purée and the Kirsch. Chop three-quarters of the canned chestnuts and stir these into the mixture. Spoon into a jelly mould and chill well.

When ready to serve loosen the jelly from the mould by dipping in hot water for a minute or two. Turn out on to a serving dish and decorate with chestnut halves and a little grated chocolate or carob.

Serve the apricot sauce separately.

The rest of the menu remains the same.

Italian Menu for Meat Lovers

Instead of the Vegetable and Almond Lasagne Verdi (page 118) do the following recipe which uses minced lamb and bacon cooked in a rich sauce similar to bolognese. This delicious meat and vegetable sauce is great spooned on spaghetti and sprinkled with Parmesan cheese. Here I have sandwiched it between layers of lasagne so I have called it Bolognese Lasagne. Traditionally, meat-based lasagne has chunks of meat and lots more cheese than in this recipe but I have added more vegetables and I think you will find it a full flavoured and deliciously satisfying main course.

Bolognese Lasagne

450g (1 lb) pasta verdi (see
  page 19)
3 tbsps cold-pressed olive or
  sunflower oil
2 large onions, about 450g
  (1 lb) in weight when peeled
  and chopped
3 large cloves garlic
700g (1½ lbs) minced raw, lean
  lamb or chicken
225g (8 oz) minced lean bacon
1 good size celery heart, very
  finely chopped
2 medium size courgettes,
  chopped

1 large green pepper, deseeded
  and chopped
2 large bay leaves
2 tbsps fresh basil, chopped, or
  2 rounded tsps dried
4 tbsps fresh parsley, chopped
2 sprigs fresh thyme, chopped,
  or ½ tsp dried
2 395g (14 oz) cans tomatoes,
  chopped with juice
2 heaped tbsps tomato purée
sea salt and freshly ground
  black pepper
1 wine glass of red wine

Batter sauce and cheese topping is the same as in the vegetarian
recipe for Vegetable and Almond Lasagne Verdi (page 118).

Follow the directions in the vegetarian recipe for rolling out the
pasta and line the ovenproof dishes as instructed.

To make the meat and vegetable filling, heat the oil in a large
saucepan and sauté the onion and garlic for 5 minutes. Stir in
the minced lamb or chicken and bacon, cook for 10 minutes
stirring from time to time. Add the celery, courgettes, green
peppers, bay leaves, basil, parsley and thyme and cook with the
lid on for 3 minutes. Add chopped tomatoes and tomato purée,
season with sea salt and pepper and stir in the wine. Cook on
gentle heat with the lid on for 15 minutes.

Follow the directions for layering as in the vegetarian recipe.
Top with the batter sauce, Parmesan and oregano and bake as
in the vegetarian menu.

The rest of the menu remains the same.

THE MIDDLE EAST

One of the most enjoyable meals I have ever eaten was at the 21st birthday party of Mohammed, a young man from the Lebanon. His doting and very caring mother prepared a feast and had it flown over for this special occasion. Each dish had little labels with a list of ingredients and full details 'to the lady of the house' on how to reheat if necessary and serve the meal. Mohammed translated these instructions for me word for word and it was just like someone talking to me a little apprehensively in case I would by accident ruin what she had so lovingly prepared for her son. I followed them to the letter and the meal was superb. Theirs was obviously a rich household but never, said Mohammed, would she let anyone shop or cook for her; it was her pride and joy. She is not unusual in the Middle East. The hospitality is renowned and even unexpected guests are offered food, and an empty plate is usually filled immediately.

That evening, 12 years ago, was the first time I tasted yoghurt cheese (see page 15), fig and aniseed preserve, chick peas and hummous. They were a sheer delight. Mohammed was overjoyed. He was so proud of his mother and his heritage.

The Middle East includes Armenia, Egypt, Iran, Israel, Morocco, Syria and Turkey. Greece, although not part of the Middle East, has a very similar tradition of cooking. All these countries are rich in grains, pulses, fruit, vegetables, herbs and spices. The most commonly used foods are rice, wheat (bulgur), black eye beans, chick peas, a huge variety of fresh vegetables, fresh and dried fruits, dates, nuts, olives, yoghurt and cheeses. The style of cooking is similar to that of India but in general hot spices are rarely used. The food is mildly spiced with lightly perfumed seasonings such as allspice, aniseed, cardamom, cinnamon, clove, coriander, cumin, paprika, orange and rose water. As in India, less meat is consumed and the diet is more varied and richer in fibre than our average Western one. Generally the dessert is fruit and nuts. The famous syrupy sweet pastries such as baklava are not eaten regularly but are prepared for special occasions only.

The menu is the result of my experiments with traditional dishes and ingredients used throughout the Middle East and Greece. You can cut down enormously on the preparation of these recipes by cooking and freezing the dried beans or peas, and rice, well in advance. See page 84 for full instructions on freezing pulses and rice. Most of the dishes can be served hot or cold so for winter or summer this menu is great.

The recipes for Maámoul (page 133) and Fig and Aniseed Preserve (page 136) are not necessary to complete the following menu. As a dessert the Sweet Spiced Apricot and Yoghurt Ice cream (page 135) and the Sesame and Ginger Snaps (page 137) are quite sufficient. I wanted to add these extra recipes because they are nice to bake and eat any time.

Middle Eastern Menu

❀ VEGETARIAN ❀

Mushroom and Rice Dolmades
(Stuffed Vine Leaves)
Imam Bayeldi
(Stuffed Aubergines)
Chick Peas with Olives
Baked Vegetable Fruit & Nut Pilau
Raw Spinach, Avocado and Tangerine Salad
Fattoush
(Breadcrumb and Cucumber Salad)
Maámoul
(Easter Buns)
Sweet Spiced Apricot and Yoghurt Ice Cream
Fig and Aniseed Preserve
Sesame and Ginger Snaps

❀

Mushroom and Rice Dolmades
(Stuffed Vine Leaves)

Makes 30

350g (12 oz) vine leaves
350g (12 oz) Surinam rice,
  soaked for 2 hours
225g (8 oz) onion, finely
  chopped
3 tbsps cold-pressed sunflower
  oil
175g (6 oz) button mushrooms,
  chopped finely
75g (3 oz) raisins or sultanas

75g (3 oz) pine nuts
3 tbsps fresh parsley, chopped
1 level tsp allspice
1 rounded tsp cinnamon
good pinch cayenne pepper
2 rounded tbsps tomato purée
sea salt and freshly ground
  black pepper
2 tbsps lemon juice

Dip vine leaves in boiling water and leave for 5 minutes, rinse under cold water. Wash the rice and cook in double its volume of fresh, lightly salted water for 15 minutes, drain. Heat the oil in a large frying pan and sauté the onion for 4 minutes, add the mushrooms and fry for a further 2 minutes. Add parsley, allspice, cinnamon and cayenne pepper and cook for 1 minute. Stir in the sultanas, pine nuts, tomato purée and rice, gently coating the rice with the mixture. Season with sea salt and freshly ground black pepper to your taste.

Place a level dessertspoon of the mixture (according to size of leaf) in the centre of each leaf, fill the bottom end of the leaf with the stuffing, fold over the sides then roll up to the top of the leaf making a neat parcel.

In a large shallow pan with a lid, place the stuffed leaves. If you have 2 layers then separate them with vine leaves. Pour in enough hot water to barely cover them. Add the lemon juice and heat to simmer. Sit a heatproof plate on the dolmades. Cover the lot with the pan lid and cook gently for about 1 hour. This dish is delicious hot or cold.

Imam Bayeldi (Stuffed Aubergines)

This delicious Turkish dish is one of my favourites using aubergines. The translation of Imam Bayeldi is 'priest fainted'. I think he must have fainted from over-eating as these are very more-ish. Just half an aubergine per person is sufficient when accompanied with the other dishes in the menu.

5 medium size aubergines, about 225g (8 oz) each
4 tbsps olive oil
sea salt and freshly ground black pepper
4 medium onions, about 550g (1¼ lbs) when peeled and chopped

3 large cloves garlic, crushed
450g (1 lb) soft, ripe tomatoes, skinned and chopped (canned will do)
1 slightly rounded tsp cinnamon
3 tbsps fresh parsley, chopped
4 tbsps chopped pine or pistachio nuts

Trim the aubergines and place in a large saucepan. Pour boiling water over them and let them stand for 10 minutes. Drain and plunge immediately into cold water, drain again and wipe dry. Cut each in half lengthwise and scoop out the pulp leaving a 1.5cm (½ in) thick outer shell, set pulp aside.

Place the aubergine shells in an oiled baking dish and sprinkle on a little sea salt and freshly ground black pepper. Spread a teaspoon of olive oil on the inside of each half and bake in the centre of the oven, 180°C/350°F/Gas Mark 4 for 30 minutes.

Heat 4 tablespoons of olive oil in a large frying pan and sauté the onions and garlic until soft, about 5 minutes. Add the tomatoes, cinnamon and parsley and cook uncovered for 20 minutes to reduce the liquid. Chop the aubergine pulp and add this with the nuts to the onion mixture and cook for a further 10 minutes, adding a little freshly ground black pepper and sea salt if necessary. Spoon into the baked aubergine shells and serve hot or cold.

Chick Peas with Olives

This is a rich dish which has lots of garlic and oil but you can cut down the amount used. It is delicious hot or cold.

450g (1 lb) chick peas
140ml (¼ pint) cold-pressed
  olive or sunflower oil
4 large cloves garlic, peeled and
  crushed
2 large bay leaves
2 tsps oregano
4 tbsps tomato purée

sea salt and freshly ground
  black pepper
juice of 2 lemons
1 medium onion, cut in very
  thin rings
20 black olives, stoned and cut
  in half
few sprigs of mint to garnish

Soak the chick peas overnight (12 hours at least) changing the soaking water 3 times, then rinse well. Put the chick peas, oil, garlic, bay leaves and oregano into a large saucepan and cook gently for 15 minutes with the lid off, stirring occasionally to coat the peas with the oil. Take off heat and add enough boiling water to cover the chick peas by about 2.5cm (1 in). Add tomato purée and blend in well. Bring to the boil then turn down to simmer, cover and cook for about 1½ hours or until the chick peas are soft. Taste and add a little sea salt and freshly ground black pepper then lemon juice.

Place in a serving dish and garnish with the thin onion rings, olives and a few sprigs of mint.

Baked Vegetable, Fruit and Nut Pilau

It is best to soak the rice for a few hours when making this dish as it is par-boiled first then baked with the other ingredients. Pre-soaking softens the grains and ensures that the rice will cook properly in the time given for baking. If left too long in the oven you will end up with a soggy mess.

75g (3 oz) dried unsulphured apricots, washed
700g (1½ lbs) Surinam brown rice
1 tsp turmeric
3 tbsps cold-pressed sunflower or olive oil
450g (1 lb) onion, thinly sliced (weight when peeled)
3 medium carrots, cut in 2.5cm (1 in) thin sticks
1 medium size red pepper, deseeded and chopped
1 medium size green pepper, deseeded and chopped
110g (4 oz) French beans, trimmed and cut in 2.5cm (1 in) pieces
1 rounded tsp vegetable bouillon powder
freshly ground black pepper
50g (2 oz) sultanas, washed
½ level tsp allspice
1 tsp ground cinnamon
75g (3 oz) split almonds
grated rind and juice of 2 oranges
few toasted split almonds to garnish (optional)

Soak the apricots overnight, chop, and reserve the soaking juices. Set aside. Soak the rice for 2 hours in cold water, rinse, put in a saucepan and add double its volume in water. Add turmeric and a little sea salt. Bring to boil, turn down to simmer, cover and cook for 15 minutes only, drain in a colander.

Heat the oil in a frying pan or wok and stir-fry the onions and carrots for 3 minutes, add the peppers and French beans and stir-fry for a further 3 minutes. Season with the vegetable bouillon powder and freshly ground black pepper. Make a well in the centre and add the apricots, sultanas, allspice, cinnamon and almonds. Cook, stirring gently for 3 minutes then add the grated orange rind, merging all ingredients gently together.

Oil a large casserole dish and layer the bottom with half the par-boiled rice. Spread on the vegetable fruit and nut mixture in a thick layer and top with the remaining rice. Measure out 200ml (7 fl oz) of liquid which includes the juice of the oranges and some of the apricot soaking water. Pour this all over the top, cover with a tight lid (it's a good idea to first cover with foil, pressing it over the edges, before putting on the lid) and bake, 180°C/350°F/Gas Mark 4 for about 30 minutes. You can leave this in the casserole dish to serve or turn out on to a shallow serving dish. Garnish with a few lightly toasted split almonds if you wish.

Raw Spinach, Avocado and Tangerine Salad

You can use crisp Cos or Iceberg lettuce shredded for this recipe if fresh young spinach is not available.

225g (8 oz) young spinach leaves, shredded
2 large avocados, peeled, stoned and sliced
6 tangerines or satsumas, peeled and sliced
4 spring onions, finely chopped
1 tbsp fresh mint, chopped

6 medium size tomatoes, thinly sliced in wedges
4 tbsps cold-pressed sunflower or olive oil
2 tbsps lemon juice
1 small clove garlic, crushed
sea salt and freshly ground black pepper

Mix the shredded spinach, avocado, tangerines, spring onions and most of the chopped mint together.

In a screw-top jar mix the oil, lemon juice, garlic, a little sea salt and freshly ground black pepper. Pour most of this over the spinach mixture. Spoon the mixture into the centre of a large shallow serving dish, arrange the tomato wedges around the edge and sprinkle the remaining mint and dressing on the tomatoes.

Fattoush
(Breadcrumb and Cucumber Salad)

This salad is a favourite in Syria. Traditionally a herb called bakli is used but as this is not available I have taken the liberty of putting in basil as it tastes really good in this crunchy mixture. Tomatoes are also normally used but I have substituted sweet red peppers. You can put both in if you wish.

2 large slices of wholemeal
  bread
juice of 2 lemons
3 medium size cucumbers, cut
  in small chunks
2 small sweet red peppers,
  deseeded and chopped
good size bunch spring onions,
  chopped
1 tbsp fresh mint leaves,
  chopped
2 tbsps fresh basil, chopped, or
  1 rounded tsp dried
2 large cloves garlic, peeled
little sea salt
6 tbsps cold-pressed sunflower
  or olive oil
freshly ground black pepper

Toast the bread on low heat until very crisp. Break the toast up
in small pieces and set aside. In a serving bowl put the lemon
juice, cucumber, peppers, spring onions, mint and basil. Pound
the garlic with a little sea salt until smooth and add this to the oil.
Season with freshly ground black pepper and pour this over the
salad, mixing it well together.

Just before serving stir in the crisp, broken pieces of toast.

Maámoul (Easter Buns)

_____ Makes 25 _____

These small pastry buns are traditionally stuffed with a dried
fruit and nut mixture. I have used the delicious Fig and
Aniseed Preserve which is given on page 136. You can
make the dough with wholemeal flour but I prefer the texture
that semolina gives to these tasty sweet treats. If making with
flour, use the same ingredients with a little less milk. Flour
dough can be used immediately but the semolina dough
must be started the night before.

MAÁMOUL DOUGH:
450g (1 lb) semolina
225g (8 oz) polyunsaturated
  margarine, melted
140ml (¼ pint) warm milk
2 tbsps fruit sugar
1 tsp rose water (optional)
pinch sea salt (optional)

little unbleached white flour for
  kneading
few extra sesame seeds to top
little warmed runny honey to
  brush tops
FILLING:
450g (1 lb) Fig and Aniseed
  Preserve (page 136)

Pour the melted margarine into the semolina mix and rub together. Add milk, sugar, rose water and salt if using. Form into a dough and knead for 1 minute. Place in a clean bowl, cover with foil then wrap a cloth tightly round the bowl and leave overnight. Next day knead the dough on a lightly floured surface until smooth (do not use too much flour). Preheat the oven to 180°c/350°f/Gas Mark 4.

To make the maámoul break off just over walnut-sized pieces of dough, roll into a ball, press your middle finger into the centre and shape into a cup. Fill with a little of the Fig and Aniseed Preserve, close up the opening making sure none of the preserve oozes out. Place each ball on to a greased baking tray, seam end down, flatten slightly and decorate the top using the prongs of a fork. Sprinkle on a few sesame seeds and bake in the preheated oven for 20 minutes. While still hot, brush with a little warmed runny honey.

These will keep for a few weeks in an airtight container.

Sweet Spiced Apricot and Yoghurt Ice Cream

I'm sure no variation of this ice cream exists in the tradition of Middle Eastern cuisine, but it would certainly be much appreciated under the hot noon-day sun in the centre of Istanbul. It can be made well in advance and defrosted to the right consistency within 20 minutes. If you want to be generous, double the quantities and make 2 moulds.

110g (4 oz) dried, unsulphured apricots, soaked in 570ml (1 pint) apple juice
50g (2 oz) raisins, soaked in lemon juice overnight
1 very level tsp cinnamon

4 tbsps fruit sugar or pure maple syrup
2 tbsps apricot brandy
350g (12 oz) yoghurt cheese (see page 15)
2 egg whites

After soaking, chop the apricots and put them with the soaking liquid into a saucepan with the cinnamon and sugar. Heat slowly until the sugar melts (stir in the maple syrup instead if you wish). Add raisins and the apricot brandy then cool completely. Purée in a blender until smooth then blend in the yoghurt cheese. Spoon into a mixing bowl. Whisk egg whites until stiff and fold into the yoghurt mixture. Freeze in a shallow container covered with foil. When thickening all around the edge transfer to a mixing bowl, beat well and place in a jelly mould. Freeze, covered with foil until needed.

Take out of the freezer 20 minutes before serving. Dip the mould in hot water, turn out the ice cream on to a serving dish and keep in the refrigerator for 20 minutes. Serve with Sesame Biscuits (page 137).

Fig and Aniseed Preserve
—— Makes just over 3 × 450g (1 lb) Jars ——

The traditional recipe for this has lots of sugar but I have added apple juice concentrate and omitted the sugar with very good results. The preserve will last for a few months if kept in a cool place or in the refrigerator. It is delicious on toast or as a filling for little tarts.

900g (2 lbs) dried figs, stems removed and washed well
575ml (1 pint) water
140ml (¼ pint) apple juice concentrate
2 level tsps ground aniseed

2 tbsps sesame seeds, roasted in a moderate oven for 15 minutes
50g (2 oz) pine nuts
50g (2 oz) walnuts, chopped

Chop the figs into small pieces. Put the water and apple juice concentrate into a saucepan and bring to the boil. Add the chopped figs and cook on a moderate heat for 5 minutes, stirring constantly. Add the aniseed, sesame seeds and nuts and cook for a further 5 minutes. Spoon into preserving jars and store in a cool place.

Sesame and Ginger Snaps

————————— Makes 24 —————————

Children as well as adults love these crispy biscuits, so make plenty. Store in an airtight tin and they will last as long as any shop-bought biscuit. These are not authentic but use the well loved sesame seeds and sweet spices of the Middle East. Make sure you use bicarbonate of soda not baking powder or the biscuits will be chewy rather than crisp.

1 heaped tsp bicarbonate of
   soda
1 tbsp hot water
5 oz polyunsaturated margarine
1 tbsp malt extract
1 rounded tsp ground ginger
1 tsp ground allspice

75g (3 oz) demerara sugar
75g (3 oz) sesame seeds
110g (4 oz) wholemeal flour
75g (3 oz) porridge oats or
   medium fine oatmeal
pinch sea salt (optional)

Preheat the oven to 160°c/325°F/Gas Mark 3.

Dissolve the bicarbonate of soda in the hot water. Melt the margarine and malt in a saucepan over a pan of hot water. Put all the dry ingredients into a mixing bowl and blend well together. Pour in the margarine and malt mixture. Mould together pressing with your hands and form into 24 small balls. Place these balls on to greased baking trays, leaving plenty of room to spread, and bake 2 trays at a time in the preheated oven for 20 minutes. Change the trays round after 10 minutes to ensure even baking. Let them cool in the trays but ease off with a palette knife just before completely hard. Once hard, finish cooling on a wire rack. Store in an airtight tin until needed.

These are delicious spread with the Fig and Aniseed Preserve (page 136).

Middle Eastern Menu for Vegans

Instead of Sweet Spiced Apricot and Yoghurt Ice Cream (page 135) do the following recipe.

Sweet Spiced Apricot Jelly

You will need a 1.7 litre (3 pint) jelly mould.

*175g (6 oz) dried unsulphured
apricots, soaked in apple juice
overnight*
275ml (½ pint) soya milk
*50g (2 oz) raisins, soaked in
lemon juice overnight*

1 level tsp cinnamon
*4 tbsps fruit sugar or pure maple
syrup*
6 rounded tsps agar-agar flakes
*2 tbsps apricot brandy (optional
but nice)*

After soaking, cook the apricots in the soaking liquid for 5 minutes, drain, reserve the liquid and chop the fruit. Measure the soaking liquid and add enough apple juice to make 1.4 litres (2½ pints) of liquid. Mix this with the soya milk. Warm the liquids and add the apricots, raisins, cinnamon, fruit sugar or maple syrup and agar-agar flakes. Bring to boil stirring constantly and cook for a few seconds until the agar-agar dissolves. Stir in the apricot brandy and pour into the jelly mould. Allow to cool completely and refrigerate until ready to serve.

Serve with Sesame and Ginger Snaps (page 137).

The rest of the menu remains the same.

Note: Vegans see note (page 140) of Moussaka recipe.

Middle Eastern Menu for Meat Lovers

Instead of Imam Bayeldi (Stuffed Aubergines) (page 129), do the following recipe for Moussaka which uses minced lamb or chicken with aubergines.

Moussaka (with lamb)

Serves 10

4 aubergines, approx. 225g
   (8 oz) each
4 tbsps cold-pressed olive or
   sunflower oil
2 large onions, approx. 200g
   (7 oz) each when peeled and
   chopped
2 large cloves garlic
700g (1½ lbs) lean minced
   lamb or chicken
395g (14 oz) can tomatoes,
   chopped
2 level tbsps tomato purée
1 level tsp cinnamon
3 tbsps chopped parsley, or
   coriander leaves
1 tbsp vegetable bouillon
   powder

1 wine glass of red wine
   (optional)
freshly ground black pepper
BATTER TOPPING:
3 rounded tbsps gram flour
   (chick pea flour)
2 eggs beaten
275ml (10 fl oz) milk
275ml (10 fl oz) natural yoghurt
½ level tsp ground allspice
little sea salt and freshly ground
   black pepper
110g (4 oz) Parmesan or
   Cheddar cheese, finely grated
   (optional)

Trim aubergines and cut in slices 1.5cm (½ in) thick. Wash slices and place in a colander, sprinkling on a very little sea salt. Cover with a plate and a heavy weight and allow to stand for 1 hour, rinse and pat dry.

Heat the oil in a large frying pan and fry the aubergine slices, a quarter at a time, briskly in the hot oil. Take out with a slotted spoon. Sauté the onions and garlic for 5 minutes (add a little more oil if necessary). Add the minced meat and fry for a further 5 minutes stirring occasionally. Stir in the canned tomatoes and their juices, tomato purée, cinnamon, parsley or coriander, vegetable bouillon powder and wine and cook on a gentle heat with the lid on for another 5 minutes. Season with freshly ground black pepper.

To make the batter topping:
Simply blend all the ingredients, except for the cheese in a liquidizer or food processor until smooth.

To assemble the moussaka oil a large ovenproof dish and spread with layers of aubergine and the minced meat mixture, ending with a layer of aubergines. Pour on the batter topping and sprinkle on the cheese if using. Bake in the oven, 180°C/350°F/Gas Mark 4 for 40 minutes, until lightly golden on top.

The rest of the menu remains the same.

Note for vegetarians and vegans:
This Moussaka is equally delicious using 350g (12 oz) red kidney beans, soaked, cooked and drained. Discard cooking liquid and proceed as above adding the cooked and drained beans just before the tomatoes etc.

For vegans you could top the Moussaka with a crumble mixture made with 175g (6 oz) wholemeal flour, 75g (3 oz) poly-unsaturated margarine and 2 tablespoons of sesame seeds.

A TASTE OF THE ORIENT

All Far Eastern cuisine, which includes Chinese, Japanese, Malaysian and Indonesian, is characterized by exquisite presentation and the use of fresh ingredients, cooked in such a way as to retain as much natural flavour and goodness as possible. Hardly any fat is used except for the occasional deep frying in such recipes as tempura (deep-fried battered vegetables) and spring rolls. As dairy herds are practically non-existent in the East, dairy produce is rarely used. Their much healthier alternative is produced from the soya bean. Soya milk and tofu (soya bean curd) both silken and firm are used extensively in cooking, so many of the dishes are suitable for vegans. The staple diet is rice, noodles and pulses supplemented with a huge variety of local fresh and sea vegetables, fruits, nuts, fish and meat. The whole attitude to food is quite different from the West. Even the simplest meals can consist of six courses and for more formal occasions you will often find at least twelve. The portions are much smaller than we are used to in the West so the bulk is probably very similar.

Particularly in China and Japan the respected cook has also to be an artist who can sculpt magnificent shapes out of ordinary vegetables like turnips and carrots. Even hard-boiled eggs are transformed into exotic gold-centred flowers and cradled on a bed of fresh green salad leaves looking much too beautiful to eat. This art is not only found in expensive restaurants but is proudly presented at most family meals. Now all this is delightful if you want to spend your life in the kitchen, which I'm sure you don't, so I have devised a menu which has a true taste of the East and is reasonably simple to prepare with just a touch of the artist here and there. My recipes are the result of much experimenting with many delicious and nutritious ingredients from the East which are becoming more easily obtainable in our shops.

You will need either a large heavy-based frying pan or a wok for the rice and stir-fry beanshoot recipes. The wok, which is a wide curved-bottomed pan, is traditionally used in China and other Eastern countries for stir-frying. It's main advantage is that the heat concentrates in the centre of the curved base and the ingredients can be pushed up the sides away from direct heat as other items are added which need different cooking times. If using a large frying pan then place on a small ring on the cooker and move ingredients to the edge when necessary. Use chop-sticks or a wooden fork to move the ingredients around.

❀   VEGETARIAN   ❀

Watercress & Leek Soup with Floating Flowers
Sautéed Tofu with Vegetables in Spiced Sauce
Vegetable Spring Rolls
Rice with Hiziki and Peas
Gado-gado
(Stir-fry Vegetables with Peanut & Coconut Milk Sauce)
Japanese Garden Salad
Lychee, Lime and Almond Mould

_____ _____

Watercress & Leek Soup with Floating Flowers

For extra nutrition and flavour use the seaweed soaking water (see recipe for Rice with Hiziki and Peas, page 147) to make up the 800ml (2½ pints) of water needed in this soup. Also, you will be using a red pepper in this menu so buy a large, longish one and trim off the solid fleshy end and cut out flower shapes with a tiny biscuit cutter or sculpt the pepper yourself.

2 bunches of watercress
4 medium size leeks, washed
  and trimmed
800ml (2½ pints) water,
  including hiziki soaking water

2 tbsps shoyu (naturally
  fermented soya sauce)
freshly ground black pepper
few sprigs of watercress and
  slices of red pepper to garnish

Wash the watercress well and reserve 2 sprigs for garnish. Chop stems and leaves. Slice the trimmed leeks in thin rings. Heat the water including the hiziki soaking liquid in a large saucepan and when boiling drop in the leeks. Simmer for 10 minutes, add the watercress and cook for a further 5 minutes. Purée the lot in a blender then push through a sieve. Reheat and stir in the shoyu and black pepper, taste and add more shoyu if necessary. When ready to serve, pour the piping hot soup into a large warm soup tureen and garnish with floating watercress leaves and thin slices of red pepper cut in flower shapes. Serve very hot.

Sautéed Tofu with Vegetables in Spiced Sauce

SAUTÉED TOFU:
900g (2 lbs) firm tofu
2 tbsps shoyu to sprinkle on
  tofu
170g (6 oz) wholemeal flour,
  plain
2 large cloves garlic and 1 level
  tsp sea salt crushed with a
  pestle and mortar
  or 1 level tsp garlic salt
¼ level tsp freshly ground black
  pepper
1 rounded tsp dried mixed
  herbs
little cold-pressed sesame or
  sunflower oil for frying

VEGETABLES:
65g (2½ oz) piece of tamarind
400ml (8 fl oz) warm water to
  soak tamarind
700ml (1¼ pints) boiling water
2 star anise
1 cinnamon stick
½ tsp fennel seed, crushed
4 cloves, crushed
bay leaf
2.5cm (1 in) piece fresh ginger,
  thinly sliced
2 medium carrots

300g (10 oz) onion sliced in thin
  rings
2 tender sticks celery, chopped
1 medium size green pepper,
  cut in diagonal short strips
1 medium size red pepper, cut
  in diagonal short strips
4 small courgettes, cut in thin
  rings
225g (8 oz) button mushrooms,
  sliced

SPICED SAUCE:
drained juice from quick-cooked
  vegetables
¼ tsp cayenne pepper
2 slightly rounded tbsps
  arrowroot
900g (2 lbs) fresh, ripe
  tomatoes, skinned and
  chopped or large tin of
  tomatoes
shoyu to taste (use the shoyu
  you marinated the tofu in)
1 tsp clear honey
2 tbsps dry sherry (optional)
little freshly ground black
  pepper
few sprigs of flat-leafed parsley
  to garnish

For the sautéed tofu:
Cut the tofu in bite-sized chunks. Spread out on a large platter
and sprinkle with shoyu, turning occasionally to coat all sides.
Leave to marinate until ready to coat and fry.

Mix flour, crushed garlic and salt mixture (or garlic salt), black
pepper and mixed herbs in a wide shallow bowl.

When vegetables and sauce are cooked, heat a little oil in a large non-stick frying pan. Dip the pieces of tofu in the flour mixture and fry quickly on all sides adding a little more oil when necessary. Drain on absorbent kitchen paper and add as directed below to sauce and vegetables.

For the vegetables:
Soak the tamarind in the 400ml (8 fl oz) of warm water for half an hour. Press through a sieve extracting as much tamarind pulp as possible and discard the hard pips. Place star anise, cinnamon stick, fennel seed, cloves, bay leaf and ginger in a piece of muslin and tie up into a small purse. Put tamarind juice, the 700ml (1¼ pints) boiling water, spice purse, onion rings, carrots, celery, peppers, courgettes and mushrooms into a large saucepan. Bring to boil then simmer with the lid on for just 4 minutes, drain, reserving the liquid in a jug. Take out the spice purse. Place the vegetables in a large ovenproof dish.

For the sauce:
Mix the arrowroot with a little of the cooled vegetable stock to a smooth paste. Blend in the cayenne pepper. Heat the stock in a saucepan. Add the arrowroot mixture to the stock stirring constantly and cook until a smooth sauce is achieved. Add the skinned and chopped tomatoes and cook for 3 more minutes stirring well. Sieve this mixture (do not liquidize) pressing well with a wooden spoon to get as much tomato pulp through as possible. The sauce will be a medium batter consistency. Stir in the shoyu to your taste, about 1 tablespoon should be enough, add the honey and sherry if using, and freshly ground black pepper, blend well together. Take out 1 cup of the sauce and pour the rest over the vegetables in the ovenproof dish. Cover with foil and leave on the bottom shelf of the oven on lowest heat to keep warm.

To assemble the dish simply heat the reserved cup of sauce. Place sautéed tofu on top of the vegetables and sauce in the ovenproof dish and pour over the cup of hot sauce, coating each piece of tofu. Garnish with several sprigs of flat-leafed parsley.

Vegetable Spring Rolls

You can buy the wrappers for these delicious deep fried rolls. They are made from tofu (soya bean curd) and called Bean Curd Sheets or Spring Roll Wrappers. Follow the directions on the packet.

8 Chinese dried mushrooms
2 tbsps cold-pressed sunflower
   or sesame oil
8 small courgettes
2 good size spring onions, finely
   chopped
225g (8 oz) bean sprouts

1 tbsp shoyu
2 tbsps dry sherry (optional but
   delicious)
1 level tsp freshly grated ginger
freshly ground black pepper
oil for deep frying
few spring onions to garnish

Soak the mushrooms in hot water for 15 minutes. Cut off woody stalks and discard. Cut mushrooms into tiny strips. Wash and wipe the courgettes, slice lengthwise into six then chop into tiny chunks. Heat oil in a wok or large heavy-based frying pan. On a high heat cook the courgettes for half a minute stirring constantly, then add the bean sprouts and spring onions and continue to fry for 1 minute. Add shoyu, sherry, ginger and a few twists of black pepper. Cook on lower heat for just 20 seconds stirring constantly. Allow to cool slightly then using a slotted spoon place 1 generous tablespoon of the mixture in the middle of each bean curd sheet. Form rolls by folding the bottom edge of the sheet over the filling first, then left and right edges over and roll the lot towards the top. Seal as directed on the packet.

Heat oil in a deep fryer or heavy-based frying pan to 180°C/ 350°F/Gas Mark 4 and fry the rolls for just 1½ minutes until golden brown. Drain on absorbent kitchen paper. Best served immediately, so give to your guests as an appetizer; they will certainly stimulate the taste buds.

Rice with Hiziki and Peas

You can prepare the rice for this dish the day before. I use Surinam brown rice as it is the thinnest variety of brown rice and quick to cook. Hiziki is a delicious strong-tasting seaweed which expands enormously when soaked so very little is needed. You can use Arame which is similar to Hiziki but lighter in flavour. Prepare the same way as Hiziki.

500g (just over 1 lb) Surinam brown rice
1 litre (1¾ pints) cold water
1 very level tsp sea salt
45g (1½ oz) Hiziki or Arame
2 tbsps cold-pressed sesame or sunflower oil

2 medium size onions, peeled and finely chopped
1 rounded tsp coriander seeds, freshly ground
1 tbsp shoyu
225g (8 oz) fresh or frozen peas, lightly cooked for 3 minutes

Spread rice out on a tray and pick over for dark brown grains which still have the outer husks on. Wash well by placing in a sieve and letting the water run through for 1 minute. Put the rice in a heavy-based saucepan, add water and salt and bring to boil, turn down to simmer and cover with a tight lid. Cook for 25 minutes, do not stir or peep, the rice will have absorbed all the water. Spread rice out on a clean tray to let steam off. (When cold you can put it in a plastic bag and refrigerate if not needed immediately.)

While rice is cooking wash Hiziki and cover with hot water then let it stand for 20 minutes. Drain, squeezing water out (reserve the juice for your soup). Heat oil in a large non-stick frying pan and sauté onion and seaweed for 12 minutes on gentle heat. Add the coriander and turn heat up to slightly brown the onion, cook for a further 3 minutes. Add shoyu and coat the vegetables well. Stir in the rice mixing it in with a light touch so that you keep the grains separate. Gently stir in the peas. Place in a warm serving dish if you have one.

Note: To make this dish into a main course you can add either 110g (4 oz) of lightly toasted almonds or perhaps 225g (8 oz) of cooked chopped chicken or prawns. Accompanied by a fresh salad this will serve 4 or 5 easily and is quite delicious for a lunch or supper dish.

Gado-gado

(Stir-fry Vegetables with Peanut & Coconut Milk Sauce)

This Indonesian dish is best cooked just before serving. You can make the nut sauce the day before and heat through just before serving.
Water chestnut is the tuber root bulb of a sedge grass grown throughout Asia. It is usually sold in tins and has a crunchy texture. You can add it sliced to any stir-fry vegetables. Dried mushrooms are expensive but they swell up when hydrated and have a stronger flavour than fresh so you need less. (To make coconut milk see page 17).

10 dried mushrooms
350g (12 oz) bean sprouts
225g (8 oz) can water chestnuts, drained
450g (1 lb) Chinese leaves
110g (4 oz) either mange tout (peas) or whole French beans
110g (4 oz) sweet red pepper, deseeded
2 tbsps flat-leafed parsley
2 tbsps cold-pressed sesame or sunflower oil
SAUCE:
2 tbsps cold-pressed sesame or sunflower oil

225g (8 oz) unsalted peanuts
½ tsp sea salt
juice of 2 lemons (about 5 tbsps)
1 small onion, finely chopped
2 cloves garlic, crushed
2 fresh chillies, deseeded and finely chopped
1 tsp clear honey
275ml (½ pint) coconut milk (see page 17)
thin slices of lemon and a few curls of fresh coconut

Wash mushrooms well and soak in a bowl of hot water for 15 minutes. Drain, discard woody stalks and slice mushrooms in thin strips. Wash bean sprouts and pat with a clean cloth. (It is important that they are completely dry.) Chop water chestnuts and shred. Trim mange tout, or if using French beans top, tail and cut into 1.5cm (½ in) lengths. Cut red pepper in 1.5cm (½ in) thin strips. Heat oil in a wok or a large heavy-based frying pan and sauté the mushrooms for 2 minutes. Add the water chestnuts, mange tout and red pepper and cook for a further 2 minutes. Stir in sprouts, Chinese leaves and parsley and cook for 1 minute more. Remove vegetables with a slotted spoon and arrange in a warm large round shallow serving dish leaving a space in the centre for the sauce bowl. Keep warm in a very low heated oven.

For the sauce:
Heat 1 tablespoon of the oil in a small heavy-based saucepan and fry the peanuts with a good pinch of sea salt for 5 minutes over a high heat, stirring constantly. Drain on absorbent kitchen paper and blend in a food processor or liquidizer with the lemon juice until smooth. Leave to one side. Add 1 more tablespoon of the oil to the saucepan and sauté the onion, garlic and chillies until lightly browned. Lower the heat and stir in the peanut purée and honey. Cook for half a minute stirring constantly then add the coconut milk and continue cooking for a further 2 minutes. The mixture should then be thick and smooth but of pouring consistency. Taste and add more salt if necessary. Pour into a small serving bowl and place in the centre of the stir-fry vegetables. Garnish with slices of lemon and a few curls of coconut (peel these off the coconut flesh with a potato peeler if using fresh to make the coconut milk).

Japanese Garden Salad

As all the other dishes for the menu are cooked, this very simple attractive raw salad is a must to freshen the palate. Traditionally salads are dressed with maybe a ginger-flavoured or sweet and sour mixture, but I prefer to accompany the deliciously flavoured oriental dishes in this menu with a very simple dressing.

1 bunch radishes, washed and
* trimmed*
2 Iceberg lettuces, about 650g
* (1½ lbs)*
1 bunch watercress, washed
* and patted dry*

DRESSING:
4 tbsps cold-pressed olive or
* sunflower oil*
1 tbsp cold-pressed sesame oil
2 tbsps lemon juice
1 tsp shoyu
½ tsp clear honey
freshly ground black pepper

To make radish flowers simply top and tail the radishes and make 6 cuts lengthwise from the base toward the stalk end with a sharp knife, leaving the last 0.5cm (⅛ in) uncut. Pop into a bowl of iced water until the radishes open out.

Wash lettuce and retain the leaves whole. Pat dry and spread out on a wide shallow serving dish placing sprigs of watercress all over the top and putting the radish flowers in the centre of each sprig of watercress. Sprinkle over the dressing.

Lychee, Lime and Almond Mould

Instead of gelatine, which is based on an animal extract, I have used Gelozone which is a vegetable jelling agent and very simple to use. You can also use agar-agar (page 23). *Double the recipe* if you want to give generous helpings to 10 or more guests.

350g (12 oz) blanched almonds
725ml (1¼ pints) water
3 tbsps skimmed milk powder
4 drops of natural almond essence
4 rounded tsps Gelozone
75g (3 oz) fruit sugar

4 tbsps lime juice
225g (8 oz) lychees (for mould) peeled, stoned and chopped finely
fresh lime slices to decorate
225g (8 oz) lychees to decorate, peeled and stoned

In 2 batches blend almonds and water in a food processor or liquidize on speed 2 (medium) for about 2 minutes then leave to stand for about 10 minutes. Strain this liquid through a muslin-lined sieve, squeezing out as much almond milk as possible. Stir in the milk powder, mixing it in well.

In a small bowl blend Gelozone or agar-agar with a tablespoon of the almond milk to a smooth paste. Stir this into the rest of the almond milk with the almond essence and sugar. Bring to boil and simmer for 2 minutes stirring constantly. Allow to cool for 5 minutes then stir in the lime juice and chopped lychees. Wet a 1 litre (1¾ pint) savarin or jelly mould with cold water, shaking off the excess. Pour in the almond jelly mixture and chill for a few hours. Turn out mould into a serving dish and decorate with slices of lime. If using a savarin mould fill the centre with lychees. If using a jelly mould then surround the edge with lychees.

Oriental Menu for Vegans

The menu remains the same except for the Lychee, Lime and Almond Mould (page 150). Simply omit the skimmed milk powder and add either soya milk powder or 140ml (¼ pint) soya milk instead.

Oriental Menu for Meat Lovers

In the Sautéed Tofu with Vegetables in Spiced Sauce (page 144), omit the tofu and add 900g (2 lbs) salmon trout or unsmoked haddock (weight when filleted).

Salmon Trout with Vegetables in Spiced Sauce
Cut the boned fish into bite-sized pieces and poach in the drained vegetable stock for 5 minutes only. Take out with a slotted spoon and arrange on top of the lightly cooked vegetables. Make the spiced sauce with what is now vegetable and fish stock water, as directed in the vegetarian menu.

You can also omit the dried mushrooms from the Vegetable Spring Rolls (page 146) and use prawns instead.

Prawn Spring Rolls   Makes 16
Follow the directions for Vegetable Spring Rolls (page 146) but omit the mushrooms and add 175g (6 oz) shelled prawns. Chop these and stir into the mixture with the shoyu, sherry and ginger. Fill in the same way as in the vegetarian menu.

Christmas Lunch

Most menus for a Christmas lunch will have an appetizing starter but personally I prefer to concentrate on giving a delicious main course and a choice of desserts which is quite enough to cope with after the usual Christmas morning drinks with family and friends.

I still do a traditional type roast dinner with all the trimmings, whether you are having a turkey or a Nut and Seed Loaf, the meal can still be a joyful and healthy one and need not take you all day to recover from.

❊   **VEGETARIAN**   ❊

———————— Serves 10 ————————

Luxury Nut & Seed Loaf (page 92)

Rich Vegetarian Gravy

Roast Potatoes

Lightly Cooked Vegetable Platter

Cranberry, Apple and Brandy Sauce

Plum Pudding

Exotic Fruit Filled Savarin with

Passion Fruit & Peach Sauce (page 101)

Yoghurt Cream (page 102)

———————— ❊ ————————

Rich Vegetable Gravy

Makes 1 litre/1¾ pints

This is a great basic stock gravy to serve with bean, lentil or nut loaves or rissoles. It freezes well so make plenty. All sorts of leftover vegetables, such as ends of red and green peppers, outside tough sticks of celery, carrots, onions, leeks, fennel etc., but I never add cabbage, sprouts or broccoli because for me these vegetables overpower and detract from the delicious, subtle taste of my stock juices. Not everyone feels the same so I'll give you my choice and you can experiment with other vegetables.

1 large onion (about 225g
    (8 oz) when peeled and
    chopped)
175g (6 oz) carrots, scraped and
    chopped
175g (6 oz) celery sticks,
    chopped
50g (2 oz) fennel bulb, finely
    chopped
110g (4 oz) mixed red and
    green pepper, chopped
1 leek, trimmed and chopped
2 cloves garlic, peeled and
    crushed
2 bay leaves

3 tbsps fresh chopped parsley
1 tsp mixed dried herbs, or 1
    tbsp fresh, chopped
1 tbsp vegetable bouillon
    powder
1 generous tbsp tomato purée
1.4 litre (2½ pts) water
1 tbsp unbleached white flour to
    every 570ml (1 pt) strained
    stock water
1 wine glass of red wine
shoyu (naturally fermented soya
    sauce) to taste
freshly ground black pepper to
    taste

Put all the ingredients, except the flour, wine, shoyu and black pepper, into a large saucepan. Bring to boil then turn down to simmer, cover and cook for about 1 hour. Strain through a colander pressing the vegetables with a potato masher to extract as much liquid as possible. Measure the liquid (to every pint of liquid you will need 1 tablespoon of flour). Blend the flour with a little cold water to a smooth paste, add a little of the hot stock liquid, blending well together. Pour this with the wine into the rest of the stock and bring to boil stirring constantly and cook for 2 minutes on a gentle heat. Taste and add a little shoyu and black pepper to your liking.

Roast Potatoes

*10 good size potatoes, well
scrubbed and cut in quarters*

*3 tbsps cold-pressed sunflower
oil*

After straining the vegetable stock and before thickening it to make the Rich Vegetable Gravy (see previous page) par-boil the potatoes in the stock water for 15 minutes. (This adds flavour to the stock and the potatoes.) Take out the potatoes and put in a colander to drain. (You can peel these if you like, but I prefer to leave the skins on.) Arrange these around the prepared Nut and Seed Loaf. Sprinkle on the oil and bake in the oven at the temperature given for the Nut and Seed Loaf. All will be ready at the same time.

Lightly Cooked Vegetable Platter

If you have any of this tasty medley of vegetables left over then simply chop and dress with your favourite vinaigrette for a delicious cold salad.

*450g (1 lb) medium size carrots,
scraped and cut in half
lengthwise*
*1kg (2.2 lbs) small sprouts,
washed and trimmed*
*450g (1 lb) French beans,
washed and trimmed (frozen
will do)*
*5 celery hearts, cut in half
lengthwise*

1 tbsp wholemeal flour
1 tsp vegetable bouillon powder
*2 tbsps cold-pressed olive or
sunflower oil*
*10 medium size courgettes, cut
in half widthwise and then in
half lengthwise*
2 cans artichoke hearts, drained

Steam the carrots until just tender, about 10 minutes. Make a small slit at the base of each sprout and steam for 7 minutes only (do not overcook or the sprouts will loose their bright green colour). Steam the French beans for 7 minutes if fresh and 5 minutes if frozen. Steam the celery hearts. Mix flour and vegetable bouillon powder together. Roll the sliced courgettes in this. Heat the oil in a large heavy-based frying pan and sauté the courgettes on moderately high heat until lightly browned. Drain on absorbent kitchen paper. Slice the artichoke hearts in half lengthwise. Arrange the vegetables in a large warm shallow serving dish, placing the cut artichoke hearts in the centre, and the other vegetables all around the edge.

Cranberry, Apple and Brandy Sauce

This sauce is absolutely delicious and can be served with many savoury dishes. You can buy 275g (10 oz) packs of cranberries in supermarkets.

275g (10 oz) cranberries
275g (10 oz) cooking apples,
   thinly peeled, cored and
   chopped (weight after
   peeling)

150ml (5 fl oz) apple juice
   concentrate
50ml (2 fl oz) water
60ml (4 tbsps) brandy

Cook all the ingredients except the brandy together for 20 minutes. Add the brandy and reheat for 30 seconds. Jar and keep in the refrigerator when cool. The sauce will keep for 4 weeks even when opened.

Plum Pudding

_____ Make four 450g (1 lb) puddings _____

3 level tsps mixed spice
1 level tsp ground ginger
1 level tsp ground cinnamon
175g (6 oz) wholemeal flour, plain
175g (6 oz) wholemeal breadcrumbs
¼ tsp sea salt
225g (8 oz) polyunsaturated margarine or shredded vegetable suet
175g (6 oz) large raisins, de-seeded

175g (6 oz) sultanas
110g (4 oz) currants
50g (2 oz) mixed peel
50g (2 oz) almonds, chopped
4 level tbsps clear honey
4 large eggs, beaten
1 large carrot, grated
1 large cooking apple, with skin on, grated
juice and grated rind of 1 lemon
juice and grated rind of 1 small orange
½ tsp vanilla essence
6 ml (4 tbsps) brandy

Mix the spices with the flour, breadcrumbs and salt. Rub in the margarine (or suet) and add the dried fruits and nuts. Stir in the beaten eggs. Add the grated apple and carrot. Finally mix in the honey and juice and rind of the lemon and orange with the vanilla essence and the brandy. Pack into four greased pudding basins and steam for 3 hours. Cover well and store until needed. Steam for 2 to 3 hours before serving.

Note on Steaming: The basins should be well greased and only threequarters full of mixture. Cut out a circle of greaseproof paper or foil larger than the top of the basin and press under the rim. Place a square of cotton sheeting over the top. Tie some string under the rim, collect the two opposite corners of the cotton square up over the top and tie together, then tie the other two opposite corners of the square to make a handle. Make sure that you have clean paper or foil and a dry, clean cloth on your puddings when storing them.

Exotic Fruit Filled Savarin with Passion Fruit and Peach Sauce
See page 101, Quartet of Exotic Fruit Filled Savarins. I think one filled savarin is sufficient as an alternative dessert to the Plum Pudding, so quarter the recipe.

Yoghurt Cream
See page 102. Half the recipe is sufficient.

Menu for Vegans

Follow the instructions for Luxury Nut & Seed Loaf for Vegans (page 108) which binds the mixture without eggs.

For the Plum Pudding (page 156), this can be easily made without eggs. Simply add 2 rounded teaspoons of bicarbonate of soda to the ingredients and prepare and steam as in the vegetarian version.

Instead of the savarin simply offer an exotic fruit salad with the Passion Fruit and Peach Sauce, (page 101), as an alternative dessert to the Plum Pudding for those who prefer a light sweet.

Omit the Yoghurt Cream.

The rest of the menu remains the same.

Menu for Meat Lovers

Omit the Nut and Seed Loaf (page 92) and use a 4.5kg to 5.5kg (10–12 lb) free range turkey (see notes on free range meat, page 21). These are becoming more easily available oven ready. Make sure you have the giblets to enrich your gravy and the heart and liver for the Chestnut Stuffing Purée.

Preparing, Stuffing and Roasting Turkey

4.5/5.5kg (10–12 lb) free range
  oven ready turkey
little cold-pressed sunflower oil
  for brushing
sprinkling of vegetable bouillon
  powder

1 recipe Chestnut Stuffing
  Purée (page 111), but use
  225g (8 oz) lean green bacon
  instead of 110g (4 oz)

Wash the inside of the turkey and wipe well with a clean cloth or absorbent kitchen paper. Stuff the body cavity with the chestnut stuffing purée (page 111), insert a long skewer through the body just below the thigh bone and turn the turkey over on its breast. Pass a long piece of string under the ends of the skewer around the wing tips, pressing them into the body firmly. Cross string over then turn the bird right side up and tie the legs together. Place the bird breast side up on a roasting tin, brush the skin with oil, place a double thickness of greaseproof paper over the breast then cover the bird with foil. To cook the bird quickly, bake, 230°c/450°F, Gas Mark 8 for 2½–3 hours. To cook slowly bake, 160°c/325°FF, Gas Mark 3 for 3¾–4 hours. Remove the foil and paper about 20 minutes before the end of cooking time.

For the gravy do the recipe for Rich Vegetable Gravy, (page 153), but add the giblets with the vegetables and proceed as in the vegetarian menu. This will be a non fat, delicious gravy and much healthier than the traditional turkey gravy which uses too much turkey fat.

The rest of the menu remains the same.

Winter Buffet Party

In summer time friends visit more often, casually dropping in just to say hello or to have a light lunch in the garden. I miss this during the long winter months which is why I love giving winter parties that bring friends together in a welcoming atmosphere. We can forget, at least for an evening, the cold dreary weather outside and brighten our lives with good food and a warming punch.

Many of the dishes can be partly or entirely prepared well in advance. Here is a list of items which if prepared before the event will ensure that you, the cook, will also enjoy the party.

The Sprouted Soya Bean Purée with Dried Mango and Ginger Sauce (page 162), can be fully prepared and frozen. Freeze in separate containers. Defrost completely and serve garnished as directed on page 163.

For the Courgette, Leek and Tomato Quiche (page 166), make the pastry base, bake blind and freeze. Fill and bake on the day of the party for best results. (You can fill the still-frozen pastry.)

The Chestnut, Nut and Mushroom Roast Ring (page 168) can be fully prepared and frozen. Defrost completely and bake as directed on page 169.

For the Curried Rice and Chick Pea Salad (page 170), cook the chick peas as instructed in the method, drain and freeze. Defrost completely. Cook the rice and let the steam off as explained in the method, allow to cool completely, pack loosely in polythene bags, lay flat and freeze. To serve, defrost completely. You can also make the curry sauce and freeze. Defrost and heat through.

For Potatoes in the Pink (page 171), make the mayonnaise a few days before the event but do not blend with the peppers and capers until the morning of the party.

For the Fresh Winter Salad with Toasted Shoyu Sunflower Seeds (page 172), prepare the toasted seeds the week before the party and keep in an airtight container.

For the Fruit and Almond Custard Sherry Trifle (page 174), make the wholemeal sponge round and freeze. It will defrost in about 30 minutes.

The Celebration or Christmas Cake (page 104), should be made 2 months before serving. Store as directed in the recipe.

The Mincemeat Slice can be fully prepared, baked and frozen. Defrost and heat in a moderate oven for 15 minutes if serving warm.

The Sweet and Sour Chutney (page 180), should be made at least 2 weeks before eating. It will last 6 months if stored as instructed in the recipe.

The Nutritious Baguettes (page 106) can be baked, cooled and frozen. Defrost while still in polythene. Sprinkle on a little warm water or milk and warm through in a moderate oven, 200°c/400°f/Gas Mark 6 for 10 minutes.

Menu

❀ VEGETARIAN ❀

Sprouted Soya Bean Purée with
Dried Mango and Ginger Sauce
Asparagus and Cheese Filo Rolls
Nori-wrapped Aubergine, Mushroom and Garlic Cocktail Bites
Courgette, Leek and Tomato Quiche
Chestnut, Nut and Mushroom Roast Ring
Cranberry Sauce (page 155)
Curried Rice and Chick Pea Salad
Potatoes in the Pink
Yoghurt, Cucumber, Mint and Coriander Raita
Fresh Winter Salad with
Toasted Shoyu Sunflower Seeds and
Avocado Vinaigrette
Fruit and Almond Custard Sherry Trifle
Warming Punch Bowl
Mincemeat Slice
Celebration or Christmas Cake (page 104)
Sweet and Sour Chutney
Choice of Six Cheeses
Nutritious Baguettes (page 106)

Sprouted Soya Bean Purée with Dried Mango and Ginger Sauce

This recipe is time consuming but well worth your efforts. Not only is it extremely nourishing but it is also a delicious blend of flavours. The mild-tasting sprouted soya bean purée has a spicy sweet and sour mango sauce swirled into it just before serving. It looks spectacular in the centre of fresh, colourful crudités. I sometimes give it as a starter, spooned into crisp lettuce leaves. However, you would have to vary the amount of ingredients according to how many you are serving at a sit-down meal.

Both the soya bean purée and the sauce freeze well so you can make this in advance and defrost completely before serving.

This recipe makes a good size bowlful. After sprouting you will have 900g (12 lb) of sprouted soya beans. For nutritional information on sprouted soya beans see page 12.

Sprouted Soya Bean Purée

225g (8 oz) soya beans (dry weight before sprouting)

3 large cloves garlic (use less if you wish)

3 tbsps fresh parsley, chopped

1 tbsp fresh mint, chopped, or 1 tsp dried

1 tbsp vegetable bouillon powder

freshly ground black pepper

To sprout the beans wash well, cover with 1.1 litre (2 pints) cold water and soak for 12 hours. Change the water 3 times during soaking then rinse and drain. Divide the beans equally and place in 2 large glass jars (old fashioned sweet jars are ideal). Cover the tops with a piece of muslin and secure this with an elastic band. Put them into the airing cupboard lying on their sides. Three times each day for 4 days pour 275ml (1 pint) of cold water through the muslin tops, shake gently and pour out all the water through the muslin. Shake the beans gently to separate and lie both jars on their sides after watering. On the fourth day the shoots will be about 1.5cm (½ in) long. If you forget to water, the beans will go sour.

When the beans are sprouted, pressure cook for 20 minutes

or cook for 2 hours in plenty of water adding a little sea salt 10 minutes before the end of cooking time. Drain, reserve the cooking water and purée the beans in a blender with the garlic, parsley, mint, vegetable bouillon powder and just enough of the reserved liquid to achieve a thick creamy consistency. Taste and add freshly ground black pepper. The purée will be a little bland but remember that you are going to swirl the rich mango sauce into it so do not be tempted to add anything else at this stage.

DRIED MANGO AND GINGER
  SAUCE:
110g (4 oz) dried mango pieces
apple juice to soak
1 cinnamon stick
1 rounded tsp fresh ginger,
  grated
½ tsp ground coriander
½ tsp ground cumin

¼ level tsp cayenne pepper
2 tbsps lemon or lime juice
1 tbsp shoyu (naturally
  fermented soya sauce)
1 rounded tsp clear honey
lemon or lime twists and sprigs
  of mint or parsley to garnish

Soak the dried mango pieces with the cinnamon stick in enough apple juice to cover, for 8 hours or overnight. Take out the cinnamon stick, drain and reserve the liquid. Purée the mango in a blender with the ginger, coriander, cumin, cayenne, lemon or lime juice, shoyu, honey and enough of the soaking liquid to achieve a smooth sauce the consistency of a thick batter.

To serve, spoon the sprouted soya bean purée into a serving bowl. Pour the mango sauce carefully into the purée swirling it as you do so with the top end of a wooden spoon, do not mix together. The contrast in colour looks great until everyone dips in, then the colours merge. Garnish with a twist of lemon or lime and place the bowl in the centre of a large flat plate. Surround with the Crudités (page 87).

Asparagus and Cheese Filo Rolls

Makes 80

These little parcels can be made well in advance and frozen.
When needed, defrost and warm through in a moderate
oven, 180°c/350°F/Gas Mark 4. They are my adaptation of
the Greek recipe which uses spinach and feta cheese. In this
recipe I have used asparagus and ricotta or goat's curd
cheese but you could use broccoli florets, lightly steamed,
instead of the asparagus. Follow the same method of
steaming, puréeing the stems and chopping the flowery tops
as in this recipe. In winter you will only be able to buy frozen
asparagus or broccoli, but both these vegetables seem to
keep their flavour well even when frozen. Tinned asparagus
is not as good as fresh or frozen.

Filo or strudel pastry comes in 225g (8 oz) packs of 20 sheets
measuring approximately 30 × 20cm (12 × 8 in), or 450g
(1 lb) packs of 20 sheets measuring 45 × 30cm (18 × 12 in).
If you have the 225g (8 oz) pack then simply defrost, unroll
and cut the rectangular block into 4 strips measuring 20 ×
7.5cm (8 × 3 in). If you have the larger pack then cut the
block in half, roll up one half and re-freeze, well wrapped.
Cut the other half in four as above. This will give you 80
small sheets.

450g (1 lb) frozen asparagus
175g (6 oz) onion, very finely
chopped (weight when
peeled)
1 tbsp cold-pressed sunflower
or olive oil
¼ tsp ground mace or allspice
1 tbsp fresh parsley, chopped
1 tsp dried tarragon
2 large eggs, beaten

350g (12 oz) goat's curd or
ricotta cheese
50g (2 oz) freshly grated
Parmesan cheese
little sea salt and freshly ground
black pepper
225g (8 oz) filo or strudel pastry
4 tbsps warmed olive or
sunflower oil for brushing filo
sheets

Steam the frozen asparagus for 6 minutes until tender. Cut off
tips, chop up and reserve. Sauté the onion in the oil on a low
heat with the lid on until transparent. Purée the asparagus stems
and the onion in a blender until smooth. Put the chopped tips,
the purée, mace or allspice, parsley, tarragon, beaten eggs, curd

or ricotta cheese and Parmesan into a mixing bowl. Stir together until well blended adding sea salt and freshly ground black pepper to your taste.

Preheat the oven at this stage to 220°C/425°F/Gas Mark 7. Brush 1 sheet of filo with the warm oil, put 1 teaspoon of the mixture about 2.5cm (1 in) from the top of the narrow edge, fold over the sides then carefully roll up. Repeat with all the other sheets. Brush the tops with more oil and place on a baking sheet about 2.5cm (1 in) apart. Bake in batches in the centre of the oven for about 12 minutes until the rolls are slightly puffed up and golden brown.

Nori-wrapped Aubergine, Mushroom and Garlic Cocktail Bites
Makes 80

Nori is a sea vegetable and comes in dry paper-thin sheets, 10 to a packet (see page 22 for more information on seaweeds in general). When dampened these sheets wrap easily around the filling. I have chosen an aubergine stuffing but you could use a mixture of cooked, mashed beans, curried rice and chopped toasted nuts or try the fillings for Nori-wrapped Sea Food and Vegetable Moulds (page 68); all are equally delicious. You can make these the day before and refrigerate until needed.

4 aubergines, each approx.
  275g (10 oz) in weight
2 tbsps cold-pressed olive or
  sunflower oil
200g (7 oz) onion, finely
  chopped
2 cloves garlic, peeled and
  crushed
50g (2 oz) dried mushrooms,
  soaked in hot water for 15
  mins.

1 tsp coriander seeds, freshly
  ground
2 tbsps fresh parsley, chopped
1 tbsp tomato purée
2 tbsps lemon juice
2 tbsps ground almonds or
  freshly grated Parmesan
  cheese
little sea salt and freshly ground
  black pepper
20 sheets of nori

Oil the aubergines and bake in the oven, 190°C/375°F/Gas Mark 5 for 40 minutes. Cut in half and scoop out the flesh, put into a mixing bowl and mash. Heat the oil in a pan and sauté the onion and garlic for 7 minutes. Cut the stems off the mushrooms, discard them and chop up the mushrooms. Add these with the coriander and parsley to the onions and fry for 5 minutes. Mince this mixture and stir it into the aubergine pulp with the tomato purée and lemon juice. Finally, stir in the ground almonds or Parmesan cheese blending well together. Season with a little sea salt and freshly ground black pepper. The mixture should be firm and stick together, if too soft and mushy then add a few toasted wholemeal breadcrumbs.

Cut the nori sheets in four so that you have 80 sheets. Dampen each one, put a heaped teaspoon of the mixture in the centre and fold over the edges to form a little pond, secure the folds with a cocktail stick. Store in the refrigerator until ready to serve. Garnish with fresh parsley or watercress sprigs.

Courgette, Leek and Tomato Quiche

This filling is sufficient for the same size pastry base, 30cm (12 in) square, as on page 94 in the Summer Celebration Menu. Square or rectangular flans are easier to cut into small portions than round ones, especially when feeding large numbers.

1 recipe for pastry, baked blind (page 94)

FILLING:
350g (12 oz) leeks, finely sliced in rings (weight when trimmed)
3 tbsps cold-pressed sunflower oil
3 medium size courgettes, sliced in thinnish rings
8 eggs
330ml (12 fl oz) skimmed milk
4 rounded tbsps skimmed milk powder
4 rounded tbsps Greek plain yoghurt

½ very level tsp ground mace or nutmeg
½ very level tsp mustard powder
¼ tsp freshly ground black pepper
¼ tsp sea salt
1 rounded tsp dried tarragon
4 medium size tomatoes
sprinkling of dried oregano and tarragon for top
225g (8 oz) Farmhouse Cheddar cheese, grated

Pat leeks dry after chopping. Heat 1½ tablespoons of the oil in a large frying pan and sauté the leeks on a gentle heat for 7 minutes. Remove the leeks with a slotted spoon. Add the remainder of the oil to the pan and sauté the courgettes on one side only until they are a light golden brown, then remove with a slotted spoon. Allow both vegetables to cool. Slice the tomatoes in thin rings. In a blender or mixing bowl, beat together the eggs, milk, milk powder, yoghurt, nutmeg or mace, mustard powder, black pepper, salt and tarragon until well mixed.

Spread 110g (4 oz) of the grated cheese on to the cooked and cooled pastry base. Spoon on the sautéed leeks in an even layer on top of the cheese. Sprinkle on 75g (3 oz) more of the cheese. Dot the top decoratively with the sautéed courgettes, golden brown side up, and the sliced tomatoes. Pour the egg mixture into a jug then carefully pour this over the cheese and vegetables, taking care not to disturb your arrangement. Sprinkle on the remaining 25g (1 oz) of cheese and a little oregano and tarragon. Bake in a preheated oven, 190°C/375°F/Gas Mark 5 for 45 minutes until golden brown and slightly risen in the centre. Cool completely before slicing.

Chestnut, Nut and Mushroom Roast Ring

You can use dried or fresh chestnuts for this recipe, personally I prefer fresh. The only successful way I have found to unstick the cooked roast from the baking tin is to line it with oven film, not greaseproof paper or foil because these stick to the roast and may break it when you pull the paper off. This is a lovely roast and can be served with gravy, roast potatoes and steamed vegetables as a traditional Sunday lunch.

The ingredients will fill 2 1.1 litre (2 pint) savarin moulds or 2 900g (2 lb) loaf tins.

Try to get lemon thyme as ordinary thyme is, I think, too strong for this recipe. If this is not possible use more marjoram instead.

1 kg (2½ lbs) fresh chestnuts or 400g (14 oz) dried
225g (8 oz) hazelnuts
110g (4 oz) pistachio nuts (weight when shelled)
110g (4 oz) blanched almonds
110g (8 oz) pumpkin seeds
225g (8 oz) wholemeal breadcrumbs
3 tbsps cold-pressed sunflower oil
2 large onions, peeled and finely chopped
1 very level tsp celery seeds, crushed

225g (8 oz) small button mushrooms, chopped in small pieces
1 level tsp vegetable bouillon powder
½ level tsp freshly ground black pepper
4 tbsps fresh parsley, chopped
2 tbsps fresh lemon thyme, chopped, or 3 rounded tsps dried
1 tsp dried marjoram
2 tbsps red wine
2 large eggs
fresh herb leaves if you have any to garnish, flat-leafed parsley will look great

Prepare the 2 moulds (sizes given above) by lining them with oven film (looks like cling wrap). Brush the film generously with oil after lining and make sure the film overlaps the inside and outside rims of the moulds. (If using loaf tins then line as you would for a cake with 2 strips of film, lengthwise and widthwise overlapping all edges.)

If using fresh chestnuts then make a small slit down the side lengthwise with a sharp knife. Bring a large pot of water to boil then simmer the chestnuts for 10 minutes, remove from heat and skin one at a time leaving the rest in the water as you do this. Cook the peeled chestnuts in fresh water for another 25 minutes, drain well and mash in a large mixing bowl. (If using dried, cover with boiling water and allow to soak for 4 hours then simmer in plenty of boiling water for 1½ hours or until soft and mashable.)

While the chestnuts are cooking lightly toast the hazelnuts in the oven by putting them on a baking tray in a single layer. Place on the middle shelf, 160°c/325°F/Gas Mark 3 and cook for 15 minutes (do not burn, check after 10 minutes). Allow to cool slightly then rub off as much of the skins as possible.

In a blender or food processor grind the nuts and the pumpkin seeds to a medium fine crumb mixture (not powdery). You may find it necessary to do this in 2 batches. Mix these with the mashed chestnuts. Stir in the wholemeal breadcrumbs.

Heat the oil in a large frying pan and sweat the onions on gentle heat with the lid on for 10 minutes. Take out with the slotted spoon and fry the mushrooms and crushed celery seeds on a moderate heat for 3 minutes, stirring from time to time. Turn up heat and reduce most of the moisture. Stir the onions back in with the vegetable bouillon powder, black pepper, parsley, lemon thyme, marjoram and red wine and cook, stirring constantly for just half a minute. Stir this into the chestnut mixture and leave to cool for a few minutes. Add the beaten eggs and mix all ingredients well together. Taste and add a little sea salt if needed. If you have flat-leafed parsley, fresh lemon thyme, or fresh marjoram leaves then lay a few of these all around the bottom of the lined and greased moulds. Carefully fill with the chestnut mixture taking care not to disturb the leaves. Press gently in, cover with foil sealing it over the edges and bake in a preheated oven, 180°c/350°F/Gas Mark 4 for 1 hour. Take the foil off and continue to bake for a further 5 minutes.

Turn out on to a serving dish. Place a bowl of Cranberry Sauce (page 155) next to the roast ring as the tangy flavour of the sauce is an ideal complement. This roast is delicious hot or cold. If serving cold then fill the centres with fresh flat-leafed parsley sprigs or watercress.

Curried Rice and Chick Pea Salad

This can be eaten hot or cold and is delicious.

225g (8 oz) chick peas (dry
   weight)
900g (2 lbs) Surinam brown rice
1 tsp sea salt
'CURRY' SAUCE:
40g (1 oz) tamarind
3 tbsps cold-pressed sesame or
   sunflower oil
2 large onions, peeled and
   finely chopped
2 large cloves garlic, peeled and
   crushed
2 cardamoms, podded and
   seeds crushed

1 round tsp ground coriander
1 level tsp ground cumin
1 tsp turmeric
1 very level tsp cayenne pepper
¼ level tsp clove powder
2 tbsps sultanas or raisins
1 cinnamon stick, broken in half
1 rounded tsp methi (fenugreek
   leaves)
1 level tbsp tomato purée
little sea salt
flat-leafed parsley or coriander
   leaves to garnish

Soak the chick peas for 12 hours changing the water 3 times if possible. Rinse and bring to boil in 1 litre (1¾ pints) of water. Boil vigorously for 10 minutes then simmer with the lid on for 1 hour or until soft. Drain well. Carefully wash rice in a sieve letting the water pour through the grains for half a minute, drain. Put rice in a large saucepan and pour on 2.2 litres (4 pints) of water, add 1 rounded teaspoon of sea salt, bring to boil and turn down to simmer. Cover the top with foil, then place lid on tightly and simmer for 25 minutes. Leave lid on for a further 5 minutes then turn out on to 2 large trays to let the steam off. This helps to keep the grains separate.

To make the 'curry' sauce:
Soak the tamarind in 220ml (8 fl oz) of boiling water for 30 minutes. Pour into a sieve on top of a bowl and press as much pulp through as possible (you will find a few hard seeds which should be discarded). Reserve this liquid. Heat the oil in a large frying pan and fry the onions and garlic for 10 minutes until golden brown. Make a well in the centre and fry the crushed cardamom seeds for 2 minutes. Blend coriander, cumin, turmeric, cayenne and clove powder with the tomato purée

until smooth and well mixed. Stir this into the onion mixture with the cinnamon stick and methi and cook stirring constantly for 2 minutes on a low heat. Add the sultanas and gradually pour in the tamarind liquid stirring well. Cook for 5 minutes on a very low heat.

Put the cooked, drained chick peas and the rice into a large shallow pottery serving dish and fork together lightly. Pour in the curry sauce, again forking it in carefully to coat the chick peas and rice well without them sticking together. Surround with fresh sprigs of coriander or flat-leafed parsley. Place the Yoghurt, Cucumber, Mint and Coriander Raita (page 172) beside it as a cooling accompaniment.

Potatoes in the Pink

Around the Christmas season you can usually buy small new potatoes which are best for this recipe.

1.8kg (4 lbs) new potatoes,
  scraped
2 celery hearts, chopped finely
2 pickled dill cucumbers,
  chopped in small pieces
1 large Spanish onion, peeled
  and very finely chopped
225g (8 oz) frozen peas, cooked
  for 2 mins. only

4 tbsps fresh parsley, chopped
PINK DRESSING:
575ml (1 pint) mayonnaise (see
  page 37)
1 good size red pepper,
  deseeded and finely chopped
2 level tsps capers, rinsed and
  drained

Steam the potatoes in 4 batches until cooked but not mushy, (cooking 450g (1 lb) at a time is best because trying to steam too many will mean the bottom layer will become too soft). When cool enough to handle chop the potatoes in 1.5cm (¾ in) chunks and place in a serving bowl with the celery, dill cucumbers, onion, peas and 3 tablespoons of the parsley. Fork gently to mix the ingredients. Blend the mayonnaise with the chopped peppers and capers until smooth and pink. Using a fork, gently stir this into the salad ingredients taking care not to break the potatoes. Sprinkle on the remaining parsley just before serving.

Yoghurt, Cucumber, Mint and Coriander Raita

2 large cartons natural live
   yoghurt
1 small cucumber, grated
1 tbsp finely chopped mint or 1
   level tsp dried

little sea salt to taste
1 very level tsp cumin seeds,
   dry roasted in a pan and
   finely ground
sprig of mint to garnish

Mix all the ingredients together except for the cumin. Just before serving sprinkle on the cumin and place a mint leaf in the centre. Place this dish next to the Curried Rice and Chick Pea Salad (page 170).

Fresh Winter Salad with Toasted Shoyu Sunflower Seeds and Avocado Vinaigrette

Prepare this refreshing salad as near to serving time as possible. You can toast and store the sunflower seeds well in advance.

Toasted Shoyu Sunflower Seeds

These are great for children's snacks and can be sprinkled on most salads for extra crunch, taste and nourishment. You need only 75g (3 oz) for this recipe but prepare lots and when cool store in a screw-top jar. Sunflower seeds are cheap and full of goodness (see page 21).

75g (3 oz) sunflower seeds

1 scant tsp shoyu (naturally
   fermented soya sauce)

In a bowl, coat the seeds with the shoyu rubbing it in with your fingers. Spread the coated seeds on a non-stick baking tray or tin and bake in the oven, 160°C/325°F/Gas Mark 3 for 10 minutes until lightly browned (put the timer on because they burn quickly). Allow to cool on the tray before adding to the salad or storing.

Note: You can do this with other seeds and nuts. For a spicy taste to serve with drinks, simply sprinkle on a dash of chilli sauce with the shoyu.

THE SALAD:

1 large head Chinese leaf cabbage, shredded (about 900g (2 lbs) in weight)

1 bunch spring onions, trimmed and finely chopped (use green ends)

3 punnets mustard cress, washed and chopped

1 large cucumber

2 large crisp green eating apples

1 tbsp lemon juice

4 medium size carrots, scraped

75g (3 oz) toasted shoyu sunflower seeds (see above)

3 tbsps fresh parsley, chopped

AVOCADO VINAIGRETTE:

6 tbsps cold-pressed safflower oil

2 tbsps lemon juice

1 large avocado, peeled, stoned and chopped

1 clove garlic, peeled and crushed

½ tsp Dijon mustard

½ tsp clear honey (optional)

1 rounded tsp vegetable bouillon powder

2 tbsps Greek plain yoghurt

freshly ground black pepper

Mix shredded cabbage, chopped spring onions and chopped cress in a serving bowl. Cut off ⅓ of the cucumber and reserve for garnish. Chop the rest into small chunks and add to cabbage mixture. Core the apples (do not peel) and chop into small chunks. Sprinkle on the lemon juice to stop the apples browning and stir into the other vegetables. Grate the carrots on the slicing side of a hard grater, you should get very thin slanting ovals, and add these with the toasted seeds (reserve 1 tablespoon for garnish) and 2 tablespoons of the parsley to the salad bowl. Mix all together and cover while you make the dressing.

To make the avocado vinaigrette:

In a blender put the oil, lemon juice, avocado, crushed garlic clove, mustard, honey and vegetable bouillon powder, process until smooth then spoon into a jug. Stir in the yoghurt and add freshly ground black pepper to your taste. Pour this over the salad just before serving.

To garnish, serrate the edge of the remaining cucumber by scraping down the skin with the prongs of a fork and slice thinly. Make a butterfly shape with one and place in the centre, arranging the other slices in a circle around the centre slightly overlapping. Sprinkle on the tablespoon of toasted seeds and the remaining tablespoon of chopped parsley.

Fruit and Almond Custard Sherry Trifle

Serves 8

This recipe is for 1 trifle which will serve 8, *so you will need 4 trifles* if you wish all the 30 guests to have a reasonable size portion.

The custard in this recipe is very simple to prepare and without eggs. Having just a few months ago catered for my son's wedding and ruined 4 trifles by curdling the egg custard, even over a double boiler, I created this foolproof version on the spur of the moment and it was delicious. Make the wholemeal sponge well in advance and freeze.

WHOLEMEAL SPONGE ROUND:

110g (4 oz) wholemeal self-raising flour

110g (4 oz) polyunsaturated margarine

110g (4 oz) clear honey

2 large eggs, well beaten

few drops vanilla essence

2 tbsps sugar-free strawberry or raspberry jam

FRUIT AND NUT FILLING:

50g (2 oz) dried mango pieces, soaked in apple juice overnight

½ good size pineapple, peeled and chopped in chunks

2 large bananas, sliced

225g (8 oz) frozen raspberries (defrost in a colander)

140ml (¼ pint) medium or sweet sherry

2 tbsps blanched and split almonds

ALMOND CUSTARD:

50g (2 oz) ground almonds

725ml (1¼ pts) milk, either goat's or cow's

3 tbsps arrowroot

2 rounded tbsps fruit sugar

few drops of pure almond extract (essence)

TOPPING:

150g (5 oz) Greek plain yoghurt

140ml (¼ pint) double cream, whipped

1 rounded tsp fruit sugar (if using yoghurt)

25g (1 oz) almonds, toasted and roughly ground (optional)

few crystallized violets (available in small packets)

angelica cut into the shape of small leaves

To make the wholemeal sponge:

Preheat oven to 190°c/375°F/Gas Mark 5. You will need a round greased sponge tin. For best results use a mixer.

Sieve the flour and reserve 1 dessertspoon of the bran to sprinkle on the sponge tin. Cream the margarine and honey until smooth and well blended. Add the beaten egg, 1 tablespoon at a time (on low speed in a mixer). Scoop out and fold in the sieved flour as gently as possible and incorporate well together. Add vanilla essence (do not beat the mixture). Sprinkle the reserved bran on to the greased tin, shake off excess and spoon in the mixture. Spread out evenly with the back of a spoon and bake in the centre of a preheated oven for 25 minutes. Allow to cool in the tin for 5 minutes then turn out on to a wire rack to cool completely. Spread with the jam and cut into pieces.

For the fruit and nut filling:

Drain the soaked mango (use the juice to make up the milk

liquid in the custard if you wish, but strain it first). Mix the mango with the other fruit, do this lightly with a fork. Pour on the sherry and stir in with the split almonds. Allow to marinate while you make the custard.

For the almond custard:
Soak the ground almonds in the milk for a few hours if you have time. Blend a little of the cold milk with the arrowroot until smooth. Heat the remainder of the milk with the almonds in a non-stick saucepan until it reaches boiling point. Stir in the sugar and almond essence, mixing well. Pour a little of this hot liquid into the arrowroot mixture and blend. Pour this into the saucepan and cook, stirring constantly for 1 minute until it thickens. Leave to cool while you assemble the trifle in a glass bowl.

Put the jam-covered sponge pieces in the bottom of the bowl. Spoon over the fruit, nut and sherry mixture pressing gently to soak the sponge with the sherry juices. Pour the custard over the fruit and let it get completely cold before topping.

For the topping:
Fold the thick yoghurt into the whipped cream and stir in the fruit sugar. Spread a thin layer of this on top of the cold custard and pipe the rest around the edge and a little blob in the centre.

If using almonds, simply toast them in a moderate oven for 15 minutes and grind to a medium fine crumb texture and sprinkle on top of the unpiped yoghurt cream area. Decorate with crystallized violets, putting 2 small leaf-shaped angelica pieces next to each violet.

Warming Punch Bowl

This is deliciously spicy and will warm your guests on a cold winter's night. You will need a 5–6 litre (9–10½ pint, capacity punch bowl.

12 cinnamon sticks, broken in half
20 cloves
2 oranges, sliced and cut in quarters
2 limes, sliced and cut in quarters
6 tbsps pure concentrated cherry juice (sugar-free)
2 tbsps pure maple syrup

5 bottles of red wine
½ bottle cherry brandy
GARNISH:
2 tbsps slivered and lightly toasted almonds
450g (1 lb) can Morello cherries, drained
3 tbsps orange peel, cut in very thin julienne strips

Put the cinnamon, cloves, sliced orange and lime, concentrated cherry juice, maple syrup and 1 bottle of wine into a large saucepan for about 10 minutes. Bring to boil on a moderate heat, remove and cover, allow to stand for 1 hour. Strain through a muslin-lined sieve. Rinse out the pan, discard the concentrate in the muslin and pour the spiced liquid back into the saucepan. Add the 4 remaining bottles of wine and the cherry brandy. Stir, warm on moderate heat but do not boil. Cover and when ready to serve heat through again, but do not boil. Pour into a punch bowl and garnish with the almonds, cherries and orange peel.

Mincemeat Slice

Makes 48 slices

The mincemeat can be made well in advance and stored in sterilized screw-top jars. The pastry for this is cake-like rather than crisp. I find it much simpler to make this mincemeat slice rather than individual mince pies when catering for larger numbers. The slice is much tastier because you get more of the filling in each portion.
You will need a 20 × 30cm (8 × 12 in) baking tray, approximately 4 cm (1½ in) deep.

MINCEMEAT FILLING: *makes 900g (2 lbs)*
50g (2 oz) dried apricots, washed
110g (4 oz) dates
110g (4 oz) currants
110g (4 oz) golden sultanas
110g (4 oz) raisins
50g (2 oz) dried pineapple (unsugared), chopped finely
50g (2 oz) dried papaya (unsugared), chopped finely
50g (2 oz) chopped almonds
3 tbsps brandy
50g (2 oz) vegetable suet (you can buy this grated)
225g (8 oz) grated apple (leave skins on)

1 tbsp each of lemon juice and freshly squeezed orange juice
coarsely grated rind of 1 lemon and 1 orange
pinch sea salt (optional)
1 level tsp freshly grated nutmeg
¼ tsp cinnamon
pinch clove powder

CAKE-LIKE WHOLEMEAL PASTRY:
375g (10 oz) polyunsaturated margarine
2 rounded tbsps fruit or demerara sugar
2 egg yolks
2 tbsps ice-cold water
450g (1 lb) wholemeal flour, plain
pinch salt

To make the mincemeat:
Steam the apricots and dates until soft, chop well. Mix all the ingredients together and store in sterilized jars if not using immediately.

To make the pastry:
Preheat the oven to 200°C/400°F/Gas Mark 6.
Cream the margarine with the sugar for 1 minute. Whisk egg yolks with the water until frothy. Sieve the flour and salt together. Add the frothy egg yolk and water with 2 tablespoons

of the flour mixture to the creamed margarine and sugar blending together. Gradually add the rest of the flour, mould together with your hands and knead for 1 minute. Chill in a plastic bag for 30 minutes.

Roll out half the dough between 2 sheets of greaseproof paper. Ease from the paper with a pallet knife and lift on to the rolling pin. Line the greased tin and trim the edges, prick the base and bake blind in the centre of the oven for 10 minutes. Turn down the heat one degree and continue to bake for a further 5 minutes. Meanwhile, roll out the other half to fit the top of the tin, again between 2 sheets of greaseproof paper. Allow the blind-baked pastry case to cool for 10 minutes before filling with the mincemeat and topping with pastry. Trim off excess pastry, fork the edges, prick the top and arrange a few cut-out pastry holly leaves and berries on top, sticking them on with a little beaten egg white. Brush the pastry top with egg white. Turn the oven down to 180°C/350°F/Gas Mark 4 and bake for 35 to 40 minutes until golden brown on top. While still hot sprinkle with a little fruit sugar or demerara sugar (optional) and cut in 6 widthwise, and 8 lengthwise, to get 48 5 × 2.5cm (2 × 1 in) slices. This is delicious hot or cold.

Celebration or Christmas Cake

Make this cake 2 months before it is needed.
See the recipe for Celebration Cake (page 104) in the mid summer Celebration or Wedding Feast Menu. It can't be improved on and will make the best rich fruit cake for Christmas or any festive gathering, but decorate it according to the season and occasion. If your winter party is around Christmas then use a decorative red and gold wrapper and place holly with red berry sprigs around the edge and in the centre. Finally sprinkle on a very thin shower of icing sugar.

Sweet and Sour Chutney

Makes 5 450g (1 lb) jars

Make this at least 2 weeks before needed. This superb chutney can be stored for 6 months in sterilized screw-top jars.

Testing it on my family the other day and in the mood for a quick lunch, I toasted wholemeal bread, spread it with margarine, put on a layer of shredded cheese, beansprouts and spring onions then a teaspoon of this chutney and toppped the lot with thin slices of Farmhouse Cheddar cheese lightly browned under a moderately hot grill. I had to hide the chutney after this.

50g (2 oz) tamarind
225g (8 oz) dried mango pieces
275ml (10 fl oz) cider vinegar
175g (6 oz) demerara sugar
450g (1 lb) medium courgettes, cut in 1cm (½ in) chunks
2 tsps black mustard seeds
1 large green pepper, deseeded and chopped
1 large red pepper, deseeded and chopped
2 large cloves garlic, peeled and crushed

2 large cooking apples, cored and chopped (leave skins on)
175g (6 oz) sultanas
1 tbsp freshly grated ginger root
1 rounded tsp freshly ground coriander
1 rounded tsp cayenne pepper
2 cinnamon sticks, broken in four
4 star anise
8 cloves
1 tsp fennel seeds

Soak the tamarind for 30 minutes in enough hot water to cover. Press through a sieve and push as much pulp through as possible. Soak the dried mango pieces overnight in this runny tamarind liquid, cider vinegar, sugar and 2 tablespoons of water. Heat a large saucepan and dry roast the mustard seeds on moderate heat until they pop. Add the mango with all the soaking liquid, courgettes, peppers, garlic, apple, sultanas, ginger, coriander and cayenne. Tie up the cinnamon sticks, star anise, cloves and fennel seeds in a piece of muslin, pop this into the other ingredients and bring to the boil then turn down to simmer, cover and cook for 20 minutes only.

Take out the muslin bag and discard. Stir the contents and spoon into warm sterilized screw-top jars.

Note: Serve the chutney with the Nutritious Baguettes (page 106), and a choice of 6 cheeses. I usually place these 3 items on a small table away from the main spread. Arrange the baguettes in a cloth-lined basket, the cheese on a large bread board and the chutney in 2 pretty serving bowls. You could also have a dish of garlic butter (or garlic margarine) if you wish.

Buffet Menu for Vegans

Instead of the Asparagus and Cheese Filo Rolls (page 164) do the following recipe.

Asparagus and Tofu Filo Rolls   Makes 80
Follow the ingredients list and method in the vegetarian recipe but omit the eggs, cheese and salt and add 50g (2 oz) Gomacio (see page 23), 350g (12 oz) firm tofu, plus 1 level tablespoon soylk (pre-cooked soya flour) blended together instead. Mix into the other filling ingredients and proceed as in the vegetarian recipe.

Instead of Courgette, Leek and Tomato Quiche (page 166) do the following recipe. The same size square or rectangular tin is needed.

Courgette, Leek, Tomato and Tofu Quiche

1 recipe for pastry (see page 166, recipe for Asparagus and Tarragon Quiche) baked blind.

FILLING:

450g (1 lb) leeks, thinly sliced (weight when trimmed)

3 tbsps cold-pressed sunflower oil

3 medium size courgettes, sliced in thin rings

700g (1½ lbs) firm tofu

½ level tsp ground mace

½ level tsp mustard powder

¼ tsp freshly ground black pepper

1 tbsp vegetable bouillon powder

1 rounded tsp oregano

1 rounded tsp dried tarragon

2 level tbsps soylk (pre-cooked soya flour)

5 small to medium size tomatoes

3 tbsps pumpkin seeds to top

little more dried oregano and tarragon to top

For the filling:
Sauté the leeks in the oil for 7 minutes and then remove with a slotted spoon. Fry the courgettes on one side until golden brown and again remove with a slotted spoon.

In a liquidizer or food processor blend the tofu with the mace, mustard, black pepper, vegetable bouillon powder, oregano, tarragon and soylk until smooth. Stir this into the sautéed leeks and mix well. Spoon this mixture into the cooked pastry case and press the courgettes golden side up in a pattern all over the top, leaving space for the tomato slices. Press the tomato slices gently into the tofu mixture and sprinkle on the pumpkin seeds and a little more dried oregano and tarragon. Bake in the preheated oven, 190°c/375°F/Gas Mark 5 for 30 minutes.

Omit the eggs from the Chestnut, Nut and Mushroom Roast Ring (page 168) and add 2 rounded tablespoons of buckwheat flour instead.

Instead of Yoghurt, Cucumber, Mint and Coriander Raita do the following recipe.

Tofu, Cucumber, Mint and Coriander Raita

Simply omit the yoghurt and salt from the vegetarian recipe and use instead 2 275g (10 oz) packets of silken tofu and 1 tablespoon of vegetable bouillon powder.

Omit the mayonnaise from the pink dressing in Potatoes in the Pink (page 171) and in a mixer blend until smooth the chopped red pepper and capers with 8 tablespoons cold-pressed sunflower or olive oil, 3 tablespoons lemon juice, 1 clove garlic, crushed, ½ teaspoon Dijon mustard, ½ teaspoon clear honey, 1 rounded teaspoon bouillon powder and freshly ground black pepper. Stir this into the potato salad ingredients.

Omit the Yoghurt from the Avocado Vinaigrette (page 173). The recipe will still be delicious.

In the recipe for Fruit and Almond Custard Sherry Trifle (page 174) use wholemeal biscuits made without eggs instead of the sponge cake. Use soya milk where milk is stated in the almond custard. Omit the cream and yoghurt topping and simply decorate the custard with toasted flaked almonds, crystallized violets and angelica cut into tiny leaves.

As suggested in the Midsummer Celebration Menu (page 104) you can make the Celebration or Christmas Cake (page 110) without eggs, but keep the mixture covered loosely with a sheet of greaseproof paper during cooking time.

In the recipe for Nutritious Baguettes (page 106) use soya milk instead of ordinary milk and omit the eggs.

The rest of the menu remains the same.

Buffet Menu for Meat Lovers

I think the only change needed in this menu is to omit the Chestnut, Nut and Mushroom Roast Ring (page 168) and do the delicious recipe for Turkey, Chestnut and Vegetable Terrine (page 111) in the Midsummer Celebration Menu. Also fill the Nori-wrapped Cocktail Bites (page 165) with seafood and vegetables.

Index